PREFACES TO UNWRITTEN WORKS

PREFACES TO UNWRITTEN WORKS

Friedrich Nietzsche

Translated and Edited by Michael W. Grenke
with additional prefaces by Matthew K. Davis and Lise van Boxel

St. Augustine's Press
South Bend, Indiana
2005

Manufactured in the United States of America.

1 2 3 4 5 6   10 09 08 07 06 05

Library of Congress Cataloging in Publication Data
Nietzsche, Friedrich Wilhelm, 1844–1900.
[Selections. English. 2005]
Prefaces to unwritten works / Friedrich Nietzsche; translated and
edited by Michael W. Grenke; with additional prefaces by
Matthew K. Davis and Lise van Boxel. – 1st ed.
p.   cm.
Includes bibliographical references and index.
ISBN 1-58731-633-1 (clothbound: alk. paper)
1. Philosophy. 2. Philosophy, Ancient. I. Grenke, Michael W..
II. Davis, Matthew K. III. Boxel, Lise van.
IV. Nietzsche, Friedrich Wilhelm, 1844–1900.
Fünf Vorreden zu fünf ungeschriebenen Büchern. English. V. Title.
B3312.E5G79 2005
193–dc22   2004030648

∞ The paper used in this publication meets the minimum requirements of the
American National Standard for Information Sciences – Permanence of Paper for
Printed Materials, ANSI Z39.48-1984.

ST. AUGUSTINE'S PRESS
www.staugustine.net

CONTENTS

Editor's / Translator's Note by Michael W. Grenke   vii

General Introduction: "A Gift for Cosima" by Michael W. Grenke   3

On the Pathos of Truth
Introduction: "Philosophy or Art?" by Matthew K. Davis   12
Text   21

Thoughts on the Future of Our Educational Institutions
Introduction: "Nietzsche's Call for Educational Reform" by
Matthew K. Davis   28
Text   33

The Greek State
Introduction: "Dignity and Decay" by Lise van Boxel   36
Text   44

The Relation of Schopenhauerian Philosophy to the German Culture
Introduction: "The Living and the Eternal" by Michael W. Grenke   60
Text   65

Homer's Contest
Introduction: "Contest and Context" by Lise van Boxel   70
Text   81

Appendix: Preliminary Drafts   93
   On the Pathos of Truth   94
   The Greek State   101
   The Relation of Schopenhauerian Philosophy to a German
      Culture   117
   Homer's Contest   126

Suggested Readings   136

Index   138

EDITOR'S / TRANSLATOR'S NOTE

This volume is a translation of Friedrich Nietzsche's book, *Fünf Vorreden zu fünf ungeschriebenen Büchern*, and of related preliminary drafts. To establish the text, I have relied upon the standard critical editions of Nietzsche's works, edited by Giorgio Colli and Mazzino Montinari, the *Kritische Studienausgabe* and the *Kritische Gesamtausgabe* (Berlin: Walter de Gruyter, 1967–).

As translator, my priority has been to provide a literal and consistent translation throughout the entirety of the work. I have taken special care in order to allow readers to discern and track connections between the five prefaces, as well as detect even rather subtle differences in the preliminary drafts of the texts presented in the Appendix. When I have found myself unable to be simply consistent, I have tried to note that in the text, and I have provided both more literal translations as well as plausible or possible alternative translations at places in the footnotes. Those footnotes are intended as aids to the understanding, and readers who prefer those translations offered there should make free use of them, both in their thinking and in any other use they should make of my translation.

As in my previous translation of Nietzsche for St. Augustine's Press, *On the Future of Our Educational Institutions*, I have translated the difficult but important term *Bildung* as either "education" or "culture," depending upon my sense of the context. Readers should freely substitute one term for the other according to their own sense. Whenever I have translated any other term as either "education" or "culture," I have included the German in brackets.

Though I included many notes for the translation, I tried to avoid including much in the notes that would impose a particular interpretation. As translator, I leave the task of interpretation to the readers. Nietzsche's writing, though it often appears readily accessible in non-technical and seemingly explicit language, is full of hidden thoughts that need ferreting out and deliberate gaps that need proper filling in. In these prefaces Nietzsche explicitly demands the kind of reader who knows how to "read the secret between the lines." As Nietzsche once put it in a brief note he wrote on style, "It is not courteous and prudent to anticipate the easier objections for your reader. It is very courteous and very *prudent* to leave it over for your reader to *express himself* the final quintessence of our wisdom" (*Kritische Studien-ausgabe*, vol. 10, p. 39).

In order to help readers begin to read more deeply into Nietzsche's texts, I have, as editor, provided both a general introduction to the work as a whole. My collaborators, Matthew K. Davis and Lise van Boxel, and I have provided separate introductory essays for each of the five prefaces. The initials of the author appear after each of these introductions. I have been lucky to have such excellent and thoughtful collaborators, and it is my hope that each of our introductions properly leads readers into Nietzsche's text in ways that will facilitate a more serious and substantial encounter with the deeper themes. Though each of us tried to understand the Nietzsche text we wrote about to the best of our abilities, our introductions should not be taken as intended to settle the matter of interpretation once and for all. Our introductions are properly best taken as provocations and invitations to further and deeper reflections.

Prefaces to Unwritten Works

A GIFT FOR COSIMA

For Christmas 1872, Friedrich Nietzsche sent Cosima Wagner a present, a slim brown volume bound in leather with metal fittings. The volume contained five essays, handwritten, numbered, put in order, and collected together under the explanatory heading "Five Prefaces To Five Unwritten Books," followed by the dedicatory address, "For Frau Cosima Wagner in heartfelt reverence and as an answer to verbal and epistolary questions, written down in a cheerful sense in the Christmas days of 1872." According to Cosima's diary, the Wagners read aloud Nietzsche's gift on the evening of New Year's Day 1873, and the matter still haunted Cosima five days later, causing her to reflect upon the nature of art.

Though moved by the work, the Wagners seem to have taken Nietzsche's gift at face value and treated it as a loose collection of preliminary material for future projects. Cosima Wagner went on to encourage Nietzsche to write two of the books promised by the prefaces. But what Nietzsche sent them is neither as loosely collected nor as preliminary as the Wagners seem to have thought. Although not really working out its arguments and suggestions in full detail, and perhaps remaining skeletal to the end, what Nietzsche sent the Wagners is a book, even if it is a book made up of sketches. And, while lacking the authority of a book put into print by a publisher, this volume has the authority of a book, made by hand by Friedrich Nietzsche himself and sent to a reader or readers whom he greatly respected and cared for.

Now Nietzsche was a man of projects. We can see this in his abundant notebooks (and to a lesser extent in his letters), which give the contemporary reader perhaps unprecedented access to the working mind of a great philosopher. Sketches, fragments, and plans abound in Nietzsche's notebooks, along with many lists of works he planned to write but never did. The five prefaces that Nietzsche wrote and put together for his gift for Cosima stand out in the extent to which they were worked over and polished (as the appendix to this volume should make clear) and in the way in which Nietzsche seemed to be thinking about them when he put his gift book together. While at one time, Nietzsche may really have written these five essays as prefaces to five separate planned books, he seemed to have come to the opinion that they truly belonged together and contributed to the understanding of each other. In a letter to his close friend Erwin Rhode on January 31, 1873, Nietzsche writes, "I am very pleased that Frau Wagner took some joy in my 'Prefaces.' You do not know them? There is a major piece in there, the first, 'On the Pathos of Truth.'" Though Nietzsche singles out *On the Pathos of Truth* for pride of place, Nietzsche also emphasizes its place in the whole.

In order to see more fully the way in which Nietzsche may have been thinking about these five essays as constituting one whole, it is helpful to consider two sketches for the plan of the work from Nietzsche's notebooks. These sketches may have been written more than a year apart, and the second may even have been written after Nietzsche sent his gift to Cosima:

> *Five Unusable Prefaces to Five Not Written Books.*[1]
> On the Future of Our Educational Institutions.
> On Fame.
> On Contest.
> On the Relation of the Schopenhauerian Philosophy to a
>   German Culture.
> On the Greek State.
>
> *Five Prefaces to Five Unwritten and Not to Be Written Books.*[2]
> 1. On the Future of Our Educational Institutions.

1   This note, labeled 8 [117] by the editors, was written somewhere from winter 1870–71 to fall 1872 and can be found in volume 7 of the *Kritische Studienausgabe*, p. 267.
2   This note, labeled 19 [327] by the editors, was written somewhere from

2. The Relation of Schopenhauerian Philosophy to the German Culture.
3. On the Pathos of Truth.
4. The Greek State.
5. The Contest of Homer and of Hesiod.

The differences in the order of the essays and in the titles of some of the essays show not only indecision but thoughtfulness. Nietzsche thought and rethought these essays, but in each case, he seems to have thought they belonged together. The titles that Nietzsche considered giving to the work as a whole seem to indicate that in Nietzsche's mind he was done with these essays.[3] Whatever the essays may have been in the beginning, by this point they were no longer to be understood as prefaces to books that were going to be written. The prefaces were "Unusable" because the books were "Not to Be Written." Instead the prefaces seemed to belong together as a book of their own, a book made of "prefaces."

But if we are to take these five prefaces as parts of one book, that is, of one whole, what is it that unifies them? Not every heap of things put together is truly a whole. We must seek the theme or themes that genuinely make these prefaces belong together if we are justly to be satisfied with the claim that they constitute a unity, one whole book. Now the theme that puts itself forward almost immediately, even to a very casual reader, is culture. Culture seems to be presented by Nietzsche as an electric chain that keeps living the greatness of geniuses of the past and prepares for and generates geniuses in the future. This presentation makes thematic not only culture, but genius, and the relation of the two. In fact this relation, in the form of the relation of one particular genius to one particular culture, appears in the title of the fourth preface. Not only that, but a word for culture appears in the title of the second preface as well, as *Thoughts on the Future of Our Educational Institutions* could have been translated with nearly as

summer 1872 to the beginning of 1873 and can be found in volume 7 of the *Kritische Studienausgabe*, p. 519.

3   It should be noted that Nietzsche did later mine *On the Pathos of Truth* for material he used in *Philosophy in the Tragic Age of the Greeks*, *On Truth and Lying in an Extra-Moral Sense*, and *On the Use and Disadvantage of History for Life*.

much right as *Thoughts on the Future of Our Cultural Institutions*. Thus one notices that the essays with "culture" in the title are sandwiched between the other essays. One might go further and see that both the second and the fourth essay describe situations in which culture is apparently lacking. The essays that sandwich the second and the fourth announce the "fundamental thought" of culture and seem to describe conditions of genuine culture that live up to that fundamental thought. These sandwiching essays, one, three, and five, all reach back to Ancient Greece, to its philosophy, to its politics, to its contests and poetry. The sandwiched essays, two and four, are set in contemporary Germany. This gives us two patterns: (1) Culture – No Culture – Culture – No Culture – Culture and (2) Greece – Germany – Greece – Germany – Greece. The work as a whole sways back and forth with an ebb and flow.

It may be that Nietzsche turns back to Ancient Greece both in order to understand the problems besetting modern Germany and to offer some hope of addressing those problems. To the "self-naming historical culture devoid of enthusiasm" that constitutes the non-culture of contemporary Germany, Nietzsche offers to "explain things, out of the most familiar times" and to bridge the "cleft of ethical judgment" between modernity and classical Greece. Just as he did in *The Birth of Tragedy*, Nietzsche sets out in these prefaces to reveal the secrets of antiquity and to show the reader the "Hellenic thoughts most worthy of noting." This may constitute not only a demonstration of culture, by showing that the greatness of the past is still available today, but it may also constitute an investigation of the character of culture, an attempt to sketch its fundamental requirements, especially its relation to and dependence upon genius. Thus Nietzsche seeks to "grasp *the Hellenic life* in its most important manifestations as a *preparation* for the highest expressions of those drives *for the birth of genius*" (*Preliminary Draft* #7). The thought that genius is the goal seems to motivate much of Nietzsche's enterprise in these prefaces:

> In the case that the genius really is the target goal and final intention of nature, thus must it now also be provable that, in the other forms of appearance of the Hellenic essence, only necessary helping mechanisms and preparations for

that final goal are to be recognized. This viewpoint compels us to investigate down to their roots much referred to conditions of antiquity, about which still no modern human being has spoken with sympathy: whereby it will emerge that these roots are exactly that out of which the wonderful tree of life of Greek art could solely spring (*Preliminary Draft* #7).

This motivated seeking out of the roots of Greek culture, a seeking out of their relation to genius, leads Nietzsche to the conclusion that "Culture . . . rests upon a terrifying ground." For this seeking out of the roots reveals something Nietzsche is willing here to call "nature," and in considering the relation of these roots to human greatness, Nietzsche concludes that "the things named 'natural' qualities and those named genuinely 'human' have inseparably grown together."

If Greek art is truly the tree of life, it seems Nietzsche pushes the inquiry in a way that risks partaking of the tree of knowledge. He asks: "Why must the Greek sculptor stamp ever again war and battles in countless repetitions, stretched-out human bodies, whose sinews are strained by hatred or by the wantonness of triumph, crooked wounded, rattling out [their] dying? Why did the whole Greek world exult at the images of battle of the Iliad?" Throughout the five prefaces, Nietzsche tries to focus the attention of "softened," modern readers on well-documented aspects of antiquity for which they have little or no sympathy. Nietzsche asks the reader to consider the necessity of war and of slavery, to see the necessity and even the positive aspects of "bloody jealousy," "murderous lust," and "tigerish triumph." High culture, and even humanity itself, it is suggested, "rests upon the greedy, the insatiable, the disgusting, the pitiless, the murderous." Nietzsche presents the Ancient Greek as reconciled to, and even approving of, such underlying human savagery. This is apparently because the Ancient Greek was aware of, or suspected, something else even more disturbing underlying that savagery, something with respect to which even war and battles seemed a "relief," "grace," or "salvation." In order to reach deep down and appreciate that something else ourselves, we "must be released from the cultural slime that now lies over all problems" (*Preliminary Draft* #13). We need to free ourselves from modernity, for the "modern human being to be sure is accustomed to a wholly other, softened consideration of things. For that reason he is eternally unsatisfied, because he never dares completely to trust himself to the fearsome, icily driving stream of existence; rather he runs up and down anxiously on the bank" (*Preliminary Draft #7*). In order to get down to the deepest problems, we need to free ourselves from our own place and time.

But in this very realization, we actually brush up against these deepest problems, for time is at least one of the names for that underlying something else that so disturbed the Greeks. Man's relation to time turns out in fact to be the deepest theme tying together these five prefaces. Culture arises as a theme only as a response to the problems posed by man's relation to time. But perhaps it is wrong to write of time as a thing that has a relation or relations to man. It may prove more correct to write of time as the relation or relations that man can have to things.

From the very beginning, *On the Pathos of Truth* announces time as a matter of deep concern for human beings who seek to escape finitude through fame or through the truth, two prominent ways in which human beings seek to satisfy their longings for eternity. In *Thoughts on the Future of Our Educational Institutions*, Nietzsche describes three qualities required in the type of readers he desires. Each of these three qualities is related to time. First the reader must be at rest and without haste; he must not consider everything in terms of whether it is "time-sparing or time-wasting." Second and most importantly, the reader must not always be interposing himself and his culture/education into what he is reading; he must be free of his own narrow time and place. Third the reader must not expect at the end new tables; he must have an acceptance of conditions of instability or motion without strictly defined order. In *The Greek State* time appears as a thing that eats savagely, like an animal: "every moment devours the one that went before." The inherent savagery of time, or its perceived savagery, may help to explain the savagery of the human's response to his temporal condition. In *The Relation of the Schopenhauerian Philosophy to a German Culture*, Nietzsche urges those who care about the people to "free themselves from the impressions that storm in upon them of that which is precisely now present day and current." Instead, Nietzsche warns the historically educated that everything "essential" lies outside of the historical approach, and "the great problems" are "unhistorical-eternal." In *Homer's Contest* Nietzsche notes that envy "warns" the human being "of the transitoriness of every human lot." And in thinking about the role of contests, Nietzsche seeks the "eternal basis of life of the Hellenic state."

Throughout these five prefaces, perhaps to a degree that current and customary opinions about Nietzsche would not have expected, Nietzsche writes of and is concerned with things like eternity, essence, and nature, things that seem to defy time and its consequences. Time, or sequence, seems to require movement, or change, and things that change cannot last. But this is very disturbing to beings who want to last. "Every disappearing and perishing we see with dissatisfaction, often with wonder as if therein we experienced something at bottom impossible. A tall tree collapses to our displeasure and a mountain tumbling down tortures us." As Nietzsche portrays it here, the human aversion to passing away is not merely displeasure at the thwarting of our desires; it is also disapproval at the breach of our moral sensibilities. Transience, time's consequence, is an injustice. In a truly moral world only things with a right to exist would come into being. But then Nietzsche asks, "How can something pass away that has a right to be!" (*Philosophy in the Tragic Age of the Greeks*, section 4)

But this is not all. In *On the Pathos of Truth* Nietzsche goes on to show that time poses yet another problem for human beings, a problem that manifests itself when human beings try to escape the narrowness of their own time and stand on the "out-stretched wings of all time." The pursuit of truth as Nietzsche presents it here is an attempt by human beings to gain access to something eternal, hence unmoving and unchanging, something not subject to the rolling of the "wheel of time." This pursuit is threatened by our love of our own, by our tendency to mingle in something of ourselves. To know a thing is not to change it. To have access to something truly is to have it as it itself is. But if we find in all our attempts to know things that something of our own is always present in the knowing, does this not corrupt our access to the truth? At the end of *On the Pathos of Truth*, Nietzsche claims that human beings are shut up within the room of their own consciousness. Do we have any way of knowing things in which our consciousness is not involved? And just what is this consciousness in which Nietzsche suggests we are locked up? At least in part Nietzsche seems to think human consciousness consists in "the representational mechanism of time, space, and causality," which seems to have the consequence that human beings "are obliged to understand everything under the form of becoming" (*Preliminary Draft* #7). As part of our representational mechanism, and thus not imposed upon us from without, time is our own and seems to mingle with everything that our consciousness tries to know. Time makes even our knowing a thing that apprehends in sequence; our knowing is a moving, changing thing that would seem unsuited to give us unadulterated access to things that do not change at all, to eternal things.

In these five prefaces, Nietzsche does a very capable job of sketching the kind of problem that time, in a variety of its aspects, poses for human beings. But Nietzsche does not leave the matter with sketching that problem. In addition Nietzsche points to a solution to the problem of time in the genius, which he associates with art and dreams. In one line of *The Pathos of Truth* Nietzsche seems to suggest that perhaps human suspicions may escape from the "room of consciousness." And it may also be the case that human beings escape the confines of consciousness in their dreams. Does art share the ability of suspicions and dreams? And if art and dreams and genius are not just arbitrary terms definable in any way whim should fancy, does not something solid and unchanging not come back into the human condition? If nature should conceal not *all* of itself, but only "most" of itself from human knowing, might there not be some kind of access to the eternal out there after all? But maybe it is not "out there" as it has so often been sought; rather could it not be found "in here"? If time is not so much a thing to which we relate but the internal way in which we have relations with things, it may offer us opportunities of mastery that have yet to be fully explored. Perhaps within ourselves and our own consciousness the powers of human making have limits yet to be defined. Time may impose its form even on our very conscious thinking, but do we not have some ability to impose our own thinking upon the form of time? Can we not project ourselves backwards into the past and forward into the future in thought in a manner that seems impossible when time is understood to be an external and material substance? In fact, the term "preface" may have its place here as the heading for these essays because of its designation of a particular temporal relation, man's projective ability to shoot forth his life into another aspect of time. Are "prefaces" man's way out?

MWG

PHILOSOPHY OR ART?

Michael Grenke tells us in the introduction that Nietzsche intended the prefaces in this volume to form a book of their own. And after one has read them, one comes away with the distinct impression that they do. One senses this perhaps because of a theme which Nietzsche announces at the conclusion of *On the Pathos of Truth* and which recurs in the essays that follow, namely, that he is heralding the outset of a new vision of culture, one whose foundation is an artistic or creative act and whose hero is the artistic genius. In order to provide its basis, though, Nietzsche must first persuade (or at least begin to persuade) his readers that the reigning version of culture, namely, that of the West, a culture whose foundation has long been assumed to be rational pursuit and attainment of knowledge of the truth, and whose hero is the philosopher, is no longer viable.[1] This is his aim in *On the*

---

1   It might be safer to say that Nietzsche does not go this far, for some of Nietzsche's remarks in the book might be taken to suggest that the (or a) main theme of the book is the tension between the artistic genius and the philosopher, and that Nietzsche understands these alternatives as rivals for the life that is, in his view, at the peak of human existence. For example, Nietzsche praises Schopenhauer, whom he calls a philosopher, in the fourth preface, *The Relation of Schopenhauerian Philosophy to German Culture,* and he speaks there of a culture that could belong to or flow from Schopenhauer. And Nietzsche concludes the third preface, *The Greek State,* by defending Plato's "perfect (or complete) state" of the *Republic,* the state in which philosophers rule, against its modern, "historically" educated, small-minded detractors. (To be sure, another important theme of the book is Nietzsche's assault on resentful, moralistic types who use "history" to level the achievements of the cultures of the past). When we

Pathos of Truth, and it may be the reason that this is the first essay in the book. For in this essay Nietzsche entertains the possibility that what really motivates those who pursue the truth – in contrast to the typical understanding that such a pursuit is a selfless enterprise – is the very self-interested aim of seeing one's fame or "one's own" last forever. As the essay unfolds, we discover that he is ultimately able to entertain this possibility because he argues that the long-held view that knowledge of the truth is possible and even attainable is an illusion. There must, therefore, be another account of why human beings, and indeed even "the rarest human beings," convince themselves that such a pursuit is real; Nietzsche proposes that they do so because they wish in some way to be "undying." Having assaulted, both by argument and

consider these examples, however, I think we discover that they suggest that my characterization of Nietzsche's aim here is closer to the mark. For I suspect that Nietzsche thinks highly of Schopenhauer because Schopenhauer argues that an act of will is at the bottom of all our action, including the pursuit of the truth, and because art occupies such a high place in Schopenhauer's overall scheme. And although Nietzsche praises Plato's "perfect state," he makes clear in *The Greek State* that Plato failed to place at its peak "the genius in his universal concept"; rather, he placed there "*only* the genius of wisdom and of knowing" (my italics). He then goes on to speak – though not entirely unambiguously – of Plato's omission of "the ingenious artist" from his state. Whatever Nietzsche's full vision may be of "the genius in his universal concept," it is clear that this genius is either not or not simply a "genius of wisdom and of knowing"; "the genius of wisdom and of knowing" does not occupy the highest rung on the Nietzschean ladder, and hence does not represent a genuine alternative to the being that occupies that highest rung. (In this regard, one might also look at what could be understood as Nietzsche's characterization of the Platonic "ideas" in the last paragraph of *On the Pathos of Truth*). I would argue that much of the evidence in *On the Pathos of Truth* and the other prefaces suggests that the being who occupies the highest rung, "the genius in his universal concept," is the artist, that is, someone whose resumé includes having the power to be a founder/creator of a culture. Nietzsche's full understanding of what the "artist" is is of course a large issue, well beyond the scope of this footnote or preface, but further study of what Nietzsche says in this book may help shed considerable light on this issue.

psychological interpretation, the West's prevailing view that knowledge of the truth is possible and even attainable, Nietzsche can devote much of what follows in the remaining prefaces to preparing the ground for, as well as sketching the outline of, a new vision of culture; he also will call up like-minded visionaries to help, and perhaps even improve, his efforts. These prefaces thus follow upon the first, and we see yet another way in which they form a whole.[2] Before we turn to

2   There are probably many ways in which the five prefaces can be understood to make up a complete book. Let me sketch more fully what I have in mind here. As I have indicated – and for reasons that will become clearer in a moment – Nietzsche intends the epistemological and psychological arguments of *On the Pathos of Truth* to help persuade us that the West's self-understanding is mistaken; he concludes by declaring that "art is more powerful than knowledge." In the second preface he calls for the reformation of the German educational institutions, those institutions that could be understood to be the most basic vehicles for promoting this new understanding. And in prefaces three through five Nietzsche begins to fill in the picture of the new artistic culture: it will be a culture that is structured politically to support the artistic genius and in this way it will be, in Nietzsche's view, closer to the Greek state (preface 3); it will be a culture that somehow embraces Schopenhauer's teaching, that will be "serious and *creative* . . . redeeming for the German spirit" and "purifying for German values" (preface 4; my italics); and it will be a culture that may again see the value in the ethics of battle and contest of the "Homeric world," that is, of a world articulated by a supreme artist who recreated a culture, whose world was "the birth womb of everything Hellenic." It is also worth noting that in this fifth preface, *Homer's Contest*, Nietzsche returns to a theme he announced in the first. He tells us that "the root of the assault" by Plato upon Homer, "the national hero of the poetic art," was, as he argues in *On the Pathos of Truth*, the lust for fame: "the monstrous lust even to walk in the place of the overturned poet and to inherit his fame." This remark alone suggests, of course, that Nietzsche intends us to think of the five prefaces as a whole work, but thinking further about the remark gives us even further reason to do so. As I have suggested, Nietzsche begins the book by arguing that the life-denying philosopher be dethroned and replaced by the life-giving vision of the artist; in the fifth essay Nietzsche restores the artist who had been most prominently dethroned by philosophy. I suggest further in this regard that Nietzsche entitles the final preface *Homer's Contest* because he wishes to emphasize that Homer the artist is responsible for the creation of the

these prefaces, however, we need look more carefully at *On the Pathos of Truth*.

Nietzsche begins the essay with the question of whether "fame" is "really only the most delicious mouthful of our love of our own." In other words, Nietzsche wonders whether the attainment of "fame" is the most desirable version of self-love that we can achieve. It is, after all, the thing sought, even lusted after, by "the rarest human beings." Moreover, in the "rarest moments" of such a human being, in his "moments of sudden enlightenments," he recognizes "the necessity of his fame." For in the moment of his insight the rare human being wishes to share his insights with others, and thinks that the insights "should remain withheld from no posterity." He believes that "humanity, right into all the future, needs" these insights. At the same time, though, and precisely because humanity for all time needs him, he feels "the necessity of his fame" and "believes himself" "to be undying."

But, since we look about us and see, to our great dissatisfaction, becoming and perishing, what will assure the reality of this belief? To guarantee that at least in some form he will not die, to guarantee the continuation of this fame, the rare individual at the height of his greatness must make the following demand: he must demand that humanity be "eternally present," and that humanity remain unchanging, so that "the great moments" will be eternally preserved and recognized. The idea of genuinely "making history" thus requires that humanity always be present to think about that history, and, moreover, that its assessment of that greatness, of the rare individual's moment of enlightenment, remain the same.

But, Nietzsche points out, "in response to the demand that greatness should be eternal . . . everything else that still lives calls out No!" Everything common and small seems to be in league against the great, trying to tear it down. The way to greatness for the great "leads through human brains," and these brains are for the most part the "brains of pitiful, short-living beings such as surrender to narrow needs," beings who "want to live, *to live somewhat* – at any price" (my italics), who both die and have little or no conception of greatness. Still, Nietzsche remarks, certain human beings strive for greatness in the face of such

ethics of contest, an ethics that Nietzsche contends gave life to and defined an entire culture.

a daunting difficulty, and they respond to it in differing ways, e.g., stoically or profoundly. Nietzsche indicates, however, that the human beings who respond in such ways, who try to "rise above" death, are ultimately unsuccessful: all of them leave "behind *one* teaching, that whoever lives life most beautifully, that one does not respect it" (Nietzsche's italics).

"The boldest knights among these fame-seekers . . . one must seek among the philosophers," "who expect to find their coat-of-arms hanging on a constellation." Having given a general account of what the rare individual who seeks fame requires, Nietzsche now turns to a particular class of fame-seekers, the philosophers. This, of course, seems an odd suggestion at first, for philosophers are largely removed from the public eye. And Nietzsche notes this. Still, even though "their wall of self-sufficiency must be of diamond" and "their journey toward immortality is more difficult and more hindered than any other," no one can be more certain "to come to the goal," i.e., fame, than the philosopher, "for disrespect of the present and momentary lies in the manner of philosophical considerations." In other words, philosophers do not look to their contemporaries for reassurance that they are and will be famous, as might a great political man; the philosopher looks to that which is presumed to be the most permanent of all, the truth. The philosopher "has the truth; the wheel of time may roll whereto it wants; it will never be able to flee from the truth." But why should we suspect, along with Nietzsche, that what underlies the philosopher's pursuit of truth is really the wish for his own, undying fame?

Having led us to ask this question, Nietzsche now provides us with an example of the philosopher: Heraclitus. Nietzsche does not cite, as we might have expected, someone more influential, such as Plato. In the fifth preface, *Homer's Contest,* Nietzsche classes Plato in the category of philosophers who lust after fame (see also footnote #2 to this essay). As we shall see, however, Nietzsche's Heraclitus does not so lust, and this may be the reason that Nietzsche focuses on him: he finds Heraclitus the most challenging figure of all. But it is odd that Nietzsche, who has been arguing that the wish for immortal fame is the real motivation for those who pursue great insights, including philosophers, should suddenly call our attention to a figure that somehow does not fit within this scheme. Why does he do so?

Nietzsche tells us that Heraclitus had no interest in his fellow man and was almost as removed from humanity as a god might be. Heraclitus's distance allowed him to think thoughts that no mortal had ever considered before – "the play of the great world-child Zeus and the eternal sport of a world demolition and a world emergence." Indeed, this distance was so great that he sought only the investigation of himself, "as if he, and no one else, were the true fulfiller and completer of that Delphic principle 'know yourself.'" Heraclitus held (or presented) the results of this self-inquiry as "wisdom," "immortal and eternally worthy of interpreting." According to Nietzsche, Heraclitus thought that his sibyl-like utterances "*must* penetrate thousands of years into the future" (Nietzsche's italics), when perhaps his wisdom will be "enough for the most distant humanity." This is so because "the world needs eternally the truth; thus it needs eternally Heraclitus, although he does not require it." Thus while Heraclitus thought the world forever in need of the immortal truth he had uncovered in his inquiry, Heraclitus understood himself as disdaining fame and the world. Heraclitus's lack of concern for fame means that in his estimation fame is not the "most delicious morsel" of love of one's own. Instead, according to Nietzsche, Heraclitus's "love of his own," or his "self-love," *is* "the love of truth." But why does Nietzsche say this? What does he mean by it? To put these questions another way, if Heraclitus' love of truth is not reducible to a wish for personal fame or immortality, why does Nietzsche still equate this love with "love of one's own" or "self-love"?

I suggest that the answer to this question is that Nietzsche thinks that Heraclitus, by loving the truth, that is, by loving something that he conceives of as permanent and needed "eternally" by the world, is still hoping that something of his will last forever. While Heraclitus may be superior to even those who desire fame, by clinging to the permanence of his truth he is still "loving his own," he still hopes that something of his, undiscovered by anyone else, will be eternal.[3] But, if this is correct, how can Nietzsche offer such an analysis of the motivation of not only most philosophers, but even of a philosopher such as Heraclitus, who is "like a star without atmosphere"?

3   The peculiarity of Heraclitus might be the reason that Nietzsche presents his initial observation about fame as a question.

Following his discussion of Heraclitus's love of truth, Nietzsche suddenly calls that love into question. He begins as follows: "Truth! Enthusiastic madness of a god! What does truth matter to human beings!" By raising the issue of whether truth matters to human beings, Nietzsche calls into question Heraclitus's assumption that "the world needs eternally the truth," and he suggests even further that "truth" itself may be no more than the "enthusiastic madness of a god." Is the god that Nietzsche has in mind here the Delphic oracle, who by laying down the challenge "know yourself" may have led Heraclitus, and indeed all philosophers, on a wild goose chase? However this may be, Nietzsche next asks the following: "And what was the Heraclitean 'truth'?" By placing the word "truth" in quotation marks, he suggests further that even the Heraclitean truth was not a genuine truth. Even the Heraclitean truth – which claims the impermanence of everything – is itself impermanent, nothing but "a dream flown away, wiped off of the mien of humanity by other dreams."

Having called into question the status of the Heraclitean "truth," Nietzsche now broadens the scope of his attack on truth. For he now envisions an unfeeling demon who reflects on "everything we name with proud metaphors 'world history' and 'truth' and 'fame' . . ." By calling "world history" and "truth" and "fame" "proud metaphors," Nietzsche suggests that these are words whose referents are gone and long forgotten, if indeed they were ever available.[4] And what does

4   See in this regard Nietzsche's discussion of truth and metaphor in *On Truth and Lies in a Nonmoral Sense,* in *Philosophy and Truth: Selections from Nietzsche's Notebooks of the Early 1870's,* edited and translated by Daniel Breazeale, pp. 79–97, esp. pp. 84–87. Nietzsche wrote this essay a year after *On the Pathos of Truth,* and even reuses passages from the latter in it. Let me quote one brief passage from p. 84. It reads as follows: "What then is truth? A moveable host of metaphors, metonymies, and anthropomorphisms: in short, a sum of human relations which have been poetically and rhetorically intensified, transferred and embellished, and which, after long usage, seem to a people to be fixed, canonical, and binding. Truths are illusions which we have forgotten are illusions; they are metaphors that have become worn out and have been drained of sensuous force, coins which have lost their embossing and are now considered as metal and no longer coins."

Nietzsche's unfeeling demon have to say about these "proud metaphors"? He reflects coldly on the clever animals on the star Earth who "invented knowledge," but discovered too late – at the point of death – "that they had known everything falsely. They died and cursed in dying the truth." But what is Nietzsche's argument for his suggestion that "truth" is a mere metaphor, that we always know "everything falsely"?

Nietzsche suggests a possible argument in the final two paragraphs of this preface. There Nietzsche describes human beings as having an "illusionist's consciousness"; we are "shut within consciousness, and nature threw away the key." In other words, if I understand him correctly, Nietzsche is suggesting that we are trapped (or nature has trapped us) within a consciousness that allows us no access to things as they are, no access to anything permanent. We are therefore constantly deceived, and ultimately have no way of distinguishing truth from illusion.[5] Moreover, we might add that if this claim is so then those in the past who believed they were pursuing truth must have been deluded, and thus a psychological account of their pursuit must be offered, and hence there may be grounds for Nietzsche's suggestion that by engaging in this pursuit they were merely, in one form or other, loving "their own."

Nietzsche, however, attempts to turn this rather pessimistic outcome into something more optimistic. Since we are cut away from truth, we should, he advises, do as we have always really done, and craft a "trustful illusion," an "achievable truth," under which we can live. Doing so might bring us closer to living and might help distance us from the "annihilation" that is the "last goal" of the misguided pursuit of truth. Grim would be the lot "of the human being if it were *just only* a knowing animal" (my italics); fortunately, we can, by means of art, craft a way to live within "the room of consciousness." Ultimately, Nietzsche asserts that "art is more powerful than knowledge," and in

5   My impression is that although Nietzsche suggests this argument here, he never stopped wondering whether such an argument is convincing. For some of his later reflections on this matter see, e.g., *Twilight of the Idols,* "How the 'True World' Finally Became a Fable," and *Beyond Good and Evil,* Part One, aphorisms 3 and 15.

the context of doing so he reminds us of the philosopher who in the "pathos of truth" tries to wake others from their dreams.[6] By believing that he can wake others, and that there is a truth to wake them up to, the philosopher merely slips into a still deeper, magical slumber, a slumber where he dreams of the Platonic ideas or of immortality.

MKD

6   I have not addressed at all the meaning of Nietzsche's title, which he surely intends us to consider. In keeping with the Greek sense of the word as well as Nietzsche's procedure in the preface, I suspect that he chooses this title because he intends to describe what lies at the core of the experience of those who think they have moments of insight into the truth.

On the Pathos of Truth

Preface.

Is fame really only the most delicious mouthful of our love of our own? – It is indeed tied to the rarest human beings, as a lust, and again to the rarest moments of the same. These are the moments of sudden enlightenments, in which a human being stretches out his arm, as if toward a world creation, commanding, drawing light out of himself and streaming out around him. There the happy-making certainty permeates him that that which raised him thus out into the most distant and whisked him away, thus the height of this *one* feeling, should remain withheld from no posterity; in the eternal necessity of those rarest enlightenments for all who are coming, the human being recognizes the necessity of his fame; humanity, right into all of the future, needs him, and as that moment of enlightenment is the epitome [Auszug] and totality [Inbegriff] of his ownmost essence, thus he believes himself, as the human being of this moment, to be undying, whereas he throws everything else from himself as dross, rottenness, vanity, animality, or as pleonasm and surrenders them to passing away.

Every disappearing and perishing we see with dissatisfaction, often with wonder [Verwunderung] as if therein we experienced something at bottom impossible. A tall tree collapses to our displeasure, and a mountain tumbling down tortures us. Every Sylvester's Night[1] lets us feel the mystery of the argument [Widerspruches][2] of being and

1   New Year's Eve.
2   Or "contradiction."

becoming. But that one instance of the highest world-perfection as it were, without a posterity and heirs, should disappear like a fleeting flash of light, offends most strongly of all the moral [sittlichen] human being. His imperative says much more: that which was *once* there, in order more beautifully to propagate the concept "human being," that must also be eternally present. That the great moments form a chain, that they, like a mountain range,[3] bind humanity through the millennia, that for me the greatness of a past time is also great and that the anticipating belief of the one lusting for fame is fulfilled, that is the fundamental thought of *culture* [Kultur].[4]

In response to the demand that greatness should be eternal, the fearful battle of culture [Kultur] bursts into flames; for everything else that still lives calls out No! The usual, the small, the common, filling all corners of the world, like heavy earthly air which we all are condemned to breathe, making smoke around the greatness, obstructing, dampening, suffocating, making muddy, deceiving, throw themselves into the way that greatness has to go toward immortality. The way leads through human brains! Through the brains of pitiful, short-living beings such as surrender to narrow needs, ever again rising up to the same necessities and with trouble warding destruction off from themselves for a trifling time. They want to live, to live somewhat – at any price. Who may suppose, among them, that difficult torch race through which alone greatness lives further? And indeed a few awaken ever again who feel themselves so blessed with a view to that greatness, as if human life were a masterly thing and as if it must be held as the most beautiful fruit of this bitter plant to know that once someone proud and stoic has gone through this existence, another with profundity

---

3   More literally, "high course."
4   Compare this sentence (*Kritische Studienausgabe* 1.756.11–16) with the following sentence from *On the Use and Disadvantage of History for Life*, section 2 (*Kritische Studienausgabe* 1.259.12–18). "That the great moments in the struggle of individuals form a chain, that in them a mountain range of humanity binds itself through millennia, that for me the highest of such long past moments are still living, bright, and great – that is the fundamental thought in the belief in humanity, that expresses itself in the demand for a *monumental* history."

[Tiefsinn],[5] a third with pity [Erbarmen], but all leaving behind *one* teaching, that whoever lives existence most beautifully, that one does not respect it. If the common human being takes this span of being so gloomily [trübsinnig] seriously, those knew upon their journey toward immortality how to bring it to an Olympian laughing or at least to an elevating [erhabenen][6] disdain [Hohne]; often they climb with irony into their grave – for what was in them to be entombed [begraben]?

7The boldest knights among these fame seekers, who expect [daran glauben][8] to find their coat of arms hanging on a constellation, one must seek among the philosophers. Their effects are not pointed at a "publikum,"[9] at the excitement of the masses and the shouting [zujauchzenden] approval of contemporaries; to march [ziehn] the street alone belongs to their essence. Their gift is the rarest and in a certain consideration the most unnatural in nature, thereby even excluding and hostile against gifts of the same kind. The wall of their self-sufficiency must be of diamond, if it should not be ruined and broken, for everything is in movement against them, human being and nature. Their journey toward immortality is more difficult and more hindered than any other, and yet no one upon [the journey] can expect [glauben] more securely than precisely the philosopher to come to the[10] goal, because he, as it were, does not know where he should stand if not upon the wide out-stretched wings[11] of all times; for disrespect of the present and the momentary lies in the manner [Art] of philosophical considerations [Betrachtens]. He has the truth; the wheel of time may roll whereto it wants; it will never be able to flee from the truth.

It is important to experience of such human beings that they once had lived. One would never be able to imagine as an idle possibility the

5 This could also mean "melancholy."
6 Or "sublime."
7 One might compare the next four paragraphs with section eight of *Philosophy in the Tragic Age of the Greeks*.
8 More literally, "believe therein."
9 Latin for "public."
10 The Kröner editions [Leipzig, beginning in 1899] have "seinem" here, meaning "his."
11 Reading Fittiche for Fittigen.

pride of the wise *Heraclitus*, who may be our example. In itself indeed every striving after knowledge, according to its essence, appears unsatisfied and unsatisfying; therefore no one, if he has not been instructed by history, will be able to believe in such a kingly self-respect, in such an unlimited state of conviction that one is the singular, made-happy [beglückte] suitor of the truth. Such human beings live in their own solar system; therein one must seek them out. Even a Pythagoras,[12] an Empedocles[13] treated himself with a superhuman esteem, indeed with almost religious shyness, but the bond of sympathy, tied to the great conviction of transmigration of souls and the unity of everything living, led them again to other human beings, to their salvation. But of the feeling of loneliness that permeated the hermit of the temple of Ephesian Artemis,[14] one can only sense something while growing cold in the wildest mountain waste. No overpowering feeling of sympathetic excitements, no desires to want to help and save, stream out from him: he is like a star without atmosphere. His eye, flaming, directed toward the inside, looks dead and icy, as if only for appearances, toward the outside. All around him waves of madness [Wahns] and absurdity [Verkehrtheit] beat immediately on the fastness of his pride; with disgust he turns away from them. But even human beings with feeling breasts avoid such a tragic mask [Larve]; in a cast-off holiness, among images of gods, next to cold, grand architecture such a being [Wesen] may appear more conceivable. Among human beings Heraclitus, as a human being, was unbelievable; and if he was perhaps seen, as he gave respect to the play of noisy children, thus had he thereby in any case considered what a mortal had never considered on such

12 Pythagoras was a highly influential Greek philosopher, born in the mid-sixth century B.C.
13 Empedocles (c. 492–432 B.C.) was a philosopher from Sicily.
14 The hermit is Heraclitus: "He would retire to the temple of Artemis and play at knuckle-bones with the boys; and when the Ephesians stood around him and looked on; 'Why, you rascals,' he said, 'are you astonished? Is it not better to do this than to take part in your political life?'" Diogenes Laertes, *Lives of Eminent Philosophers,* IX.3, (*Life of Heraclitus*); R. D. Hicks, translator (slightly modified); Cambridge: Harvard University Press, 1965.

an occasion – the play of the great world-child Zeus[15] and the eternal sport[16] of a world demolition and a world emergence. He did not need human beings, not even for his knowledge; there lay nothing for him in everything which one could possibly ask of them and which the other wise ones before him had bothered to ask. "I sought and investigated myself,"[17] he said with a phrase [Worte] by which one designated the investigation of an oracle:[18] as if he, and no one else, were the true fulfiller and completer of that Delphic principle, "know yourself."

But what he heard from this oracle he held for wisdom, immortal and eternally worthy of interpreting, in the sense in which the prophetic speeches of the Sibyl are immortal. It is enough for the most distant humanity: may they interpret it only as oracular speech, as he, like the Delphic god himself, "neither says, nor conceals."[19] Similarly, if it is proclaimed by him "without laughing, without finery and scented ointment," much more as with "foaming mouth," it *must* penetrate thousands of years into the future.[20] For the world needs eternally the truth; thus it needs eternally Heraclitus, although he does not require it. What does his fame matter to *him*! "Fame with ever-flowing-away

15 See *Philosophy in the Tragic Age of the Greeks*, section 6; cf. Heraclitus Fragment 52.

16 Or "joke."

17 Diogenes Laertes, *Lives*, IX.5 (*Life of Heraclitus*): ἤκουσέ τ᾽ οὐδενος, ἀλλ᾽ αὑτὸν ἔφη διζήσαθαι καὶ μαθεῖν πάντα παρ᾽ εάτοῦ. "He was the pupil of no one, but said that he 'inquired of himself' and learned everything from himself"; cf. Heraclitus Fragment 101, ἐδιζησάμην ἐμεωυτόν "I investigated myself."

18 The verb δίζημαι is a rather rare word, meaning "seeking out" and is often used with respect to seeking out the meaning of prophets and their prophecies.

19 Heraclitus Fragment 93: ὁ ἄναξ, οὗ τὸ μαντεῖον ἐστι τὸ ἐν Δελφοῖς, οὔτε λέγει οὔτε κρύπτει ἀλλὰ σημαίνει "The lord, the oracle of whom is in Delphi neither says nor conceals but gives a sign."

20 Heraclitus Fragment 92: Σίβυλλα δὲ μαινομένωι στόματι καθ᾽ Ἡράκλειτου ἀγέλαστα καὶ ἀκαλλώπιστα καὶ ἀμύριστα φθεγγομένη χιλίων ἐτῶν ἐξικνεῖται τῆι φωνῆι διὰ τὸν θεόν. "But the Sibyl raging in the mouth, according to Heraclitus, uttering words without laughter, unadorned and without fragrances, reaches us with clarity a thousand years later, by means of the god."

mortals!"[21] as he mockingly exclaimed. That is something for singers and poets, also for those who had been known before him as "wise" men – these may gobble up the most delicious morsel of their love of their own; for him this meal is too common. His fame matters somewhat to human beings, not to him; his love of his own is the love of truth – and just this truth says to him that the immortality of humanity needs him, not that he needs the immortality of the human being Heraclitus.

Truth! Enthusiastic madness of a god! What does truth matter to human beings!

And what was the Heraclitean "truth"!

And where has it gone? A dream flown away, wiped off the mien of humanity by other dreams! – It was not the first!

Perhaps a demon, devoid of feeling, would have nothing to say of everything that we name with proud metaphors "world history" and "truth" and "fame" other than these words:

"In some remote corner of the universe filled up with countless solar systems twinkling there was once a star [Gestirn][22] on which clever animals invented *knowledge*.[23] It was the most arrogant [hochmüthigste] and most lying minute of world history, but still only one minute. After a few courses of the breath of nature the star grew cold, and the clever animals had to die. It was also in time; for if they already boasted to have known much, they had finally seen behind that, to their great crossness, the fact that they had known everything falsely. They died and cursed in dying the truth. That was the way [Art] of these desperate animals, who had discovered knowledge."

This would be the lot of the human being if it were just only a knowing animal; truth would drive it to despair and to annihilation,

---

21 Heraclitus Fragment 29: αἱρεῦνται γὰρ ἕν ἀντὶ ἁπάντων οἱ ἄριστοι, κλέος ἀέναον θνητῶν· οἱ δὲ πολλοὶ κεκόρηνται ὅκωσπερ κτήνεα. "For the best take one thing in opposition to everything else, glory ever flowing among mortals. But the many are glutted like herds."
22 This was translated earlier as "constellation."
23 The beginning of this paragraph was used verbatim by Nietzsche for the first seven lines of *On Truth and Lying in an Extramoral Sense*. The punctuation is a little different there, and "world history" is in quotation marks.

truth, to be eternally condemned to untruth. But to the human being is fitting alone the belief in achievable truth, in the trustful illusion drawing near to him. Does he not live authentically *through* a continuous becoming deceived? Does not nature conceal from him most things [Allermeiste], indeed precisely the nearest [Allernächste], e.g., his own body, of which he only has an illusionist's [gauklerisches] "consciousness"? He is shut in within this consciousness, and nature threw away the key. Oh the fatal [Verhängnißvoll] curiosity of the philosopher, who longs for once to look out and down through a crack out of the room of consciousness: perhaps then he suspects how the human being rests upon the greedy, the insatiable, the disgusting, the pitiless, the murderous, in the indifference of his not knowing and, as it were, hanging upon the back of a tiger in dreams.

"Let him hang," calls art. "Wake him up," calls the philosopher in the pathos of truth. Indeed, while he believes himself to shake the sleeping one, he himself sinks down into a still deeper, magical slumber – perhaps he dreams then of the "ideas" or of immortality. Art is more powerful than knowledge, for *the former* wants life and the latter achieves as a last goal only – annihilation.

NIETZSCHE'S CALL FOR EDUCATIONAL REFORM

This preface is a revised version of the preface to the set of lectures that constitute Nietzsche's unpublished work, *On the Future of Our Educational Institutions*. Nietzsche remarks there that "although [the preface] does not genuinely apply" to the lectures, "it is to be read before" them. He may therefore intend the preface to be a kind of inspirational prelude, and, if so, it would also fill the place that I have suggested in my introduction to *On the Pathos of Truth* – it would be part of the invocation and sketch of Nietzsche's new project for, or vision of, culture that is a main theme of this book. And it makes sense that this new project would begin with an inspirational call for the reform of educational institutions, since reform of education is often thought of in our time as the beginning point both for the reform and promotion of culture. Early on in this preface Nietzsche says the following: "I daresay I see a time coming, in which serious human beings, in the service of a fully renewed and purified culture and in common labor, even again become the legislators of everyday education – of education toward just that culture . . ."[1]

That Nietzsche begins here may tell us something about Nietzsche himself. For Nietzsche's first step in his new project of reformation is not reformation of political institutions but of educational institutions. He addresses political issues after educational issues (see *The Greek State*). In this sense Nietzsche seems very much a modern. He does not

1   In the original version of the preface, in place of "toward just that culture" Nietzsche says "toward that new culture."

think of political things as fundamental; he does not think of the city as coeval with human life and hence as providing the fundamental education for human beings; rather he understands education as a basic and separate component of a culture that is formed (and reformed) by human beings. Nietzsche, in a remark that he adds to this revised preface, says that a reader who is of the opinion that with a new "'organization' by the state" he can reach the goal Nietzsche sees only dimly in the distance has "understood neither the author nor the authentic problem." But what is "the authentic problem"? Perhaps we will find out by examining the preface more closely.

Nietzsche begins this preface by listing the qualities that his readers – that is, readers who might understand him – must have. This preface, as we have suggested, is thus a call to a certain kind of reader. First, this reader must "be at rest and read without haste." Second, he must not always "be bringing himself and his education in between." Finally, he should not "expect at the conclusion, as a result for instance, tables." In the course of the preface, Nietzsche does not take up these qualities in order. Instead, he addresses the third quality first, and the second quality – which he identifies as most important – last. Nietzsche states in the first sentence of the preface that he expects something from his reader; he adds later that this reader will not have "unlearned to think while he reads" but will still be able "to read the secret between the lines." By taking up the qualities of his reader in a different order, Nietzsche may indicate something about the attentiveness he requires of his reader, namely, that the reader should consider the order of his examples: the most important example may not be the first one that he lists, but rather the central example. We shall see whether we can determine why Nietzsche thinks the second quality most important.

Nietzsche then turns to his requirement that his reader not "expect at the conclusion, as a result for instance, tables." What does he mean by this requirement? He remarks further that "tables and new curricula for Gymnasiums and other schools I do not promise . . ." Nietzsche thus has something much larger in mind than, say, a five-hundred-page document on how we reform the current state of our schools to better serve all our schoolchildren; Nietzsche's aim is not to reform the current system from within. While he marvels at those who can "traverse the whole way, from out of the depths of empiricism up to the heights of the genuine problems of culture and again down from there into the lowlands of the driest regulations and of the most elegant works of tables," Nietzsche is content himself to have climbed "a passable mountain" where he delights "over the free view." Nietzsche thus implies that one begins one's trip from "the depths of empiricism," from the modern, methodical scientific and social scientific procedure that produces five-hundred-page documents of regulations and tables. Nietzsche, however, does not take the whole trip, but stays at the top of the mountain, considering, we gather, "the genuine problems of culture."[2] From this "free view," from the place where he has transcended the current culture, Nietzsche can see, as we have noted, the time when "serious human beings, in service of a fully renewed and purified culture," become legislators of education for that culture. Nietzsche does not discount the possibility that at that time these new legislators will make "tables," but this is only after Nietzsche finds his deepest readers and they carry out, perhaps among other things, what Nietzsche calls the "annihilation" or "total reformation" of the present educational institutions.

Having called upon the reader who will rise above the "empiricist" approach to education, Nietzsche turns to the quality initially listed first. Again, he wishes for a reader that is not caught up in the "time-sparing or time-wasting" attitude of the modern age, that is, we suspect, in what we might characterize as the driven, self-interested attitude of the modern *bourgeois*. This seems to go hand-in-glove with Nietzsche's rejection of empiricism, that is, of the modern scientific approach that accompanies and helps promote the *bourgeois* way of life. (It also goes along with his rejection of "'organization' by the state" in order to solve educational problems, of the kinds of "reorganizations" that make "education" available to the greatest possible number so that there can be even more *bourgeoisie*). Instead, Nietzsche's call is to readers who "still have time" "to reflect on the future of our education." As Nietzsche will also stress in his discussion

2   Nietzsche may also intend his references here to climbing up and staying on the mountain and to tables to remind us of Moses and the two tables of the Decalogue.

of the third quality, these readers must be readers who are not interested in the "idolatrous pleasure" of the fun of "our rolling age" but who
are willing to believe in something higher. The higher thing in question
is not any particular religion but the vision, however limited, of
Nietzsche himself: "You are my reader, for you are calm enough to be
able to set out together on a distant way with the author, whose goal he
cannot see, in whose goal he must honestly believe, in order that later,
perhaps a distant generation should see with its eyes, where we, blind
and only led by instinct, grope."[3]

Nietzsche continues this theme in his discussion of the final quality needed in his reader. This reader may not, "after the manner of the
modern human being, be permitted to bring himself and his education
without pause, for instance as a measuring stick, in between as if with
that he would possess a criterion of all things." Nietzsche again calls
into question the modern, bourgeois, empiricist approach to things.
This education must be put aside so that the reader may "with the
greatest trust surrender himself to the leading of his author."[4]
Nietzsche may think this quality in his reader most important because
it requires his reader to do what Nietzsche has done, namely, to stand
apart from or above his own education and "despise it," to take the
measure of the "strongly excited feeling" he has "for the specific character of our German barbarism, for that which so designates us as the
barbarians of the nineteenth century . . ."[5] But why should the reader
do this?

3   This statement differs in the original version of the preface. There
      Nietzsche says the following of his reader: "He who is calm and uncon-
      cerned enough to be able to set out together on a distant way with the
      author, whose goal will first be shown in full clarity to a much later gen-
      eration!" In the revised version Nietzsche seems to request of his reader
      even more trust and sacrifice than he requested in his original version of
      the preface.
4   I note in this regard that modern empiricism is a perfect companion for
      the modern bourgeois attitude of self-interest and distrust, for a funda-
      mental premise of modern empiricism is a distrust of the world as it pres-
      ents itself, a distrust that makes possible the conquest of nature.
5   The original version of the preface reads "present German barbarism."

This question may ask too much from a preface that is, as we have suggested, intended as a vehicle of inspiration. And Nietzsche stresses the need for his reader, in putting his education behind him, to surrender himself "with the greatest trust" to Nietzsche's leadership. Still, Nietzsche does mention, in passing, his qualifications for leadership in crafting the beginnings of a new, more noble culture: his reader may "surrender himself to the leading of the author, to whom it is permitted to dare, exactly from not-knowing and from knowledge about not-knowing, to speak to him." In other words, Nietzsche seems to suggest that it is precisely his critique of knowledge and truth – that is, the kind of critique that we find in *On the Pathos of Truth* – that qualifies him to address and call up his new reader.[6] If this is so, perhaps I have put my finger on what Nietzsche refers to earlier as "the authentic problem," and on the insight that he believes allows him to transcend not only modern culture but also the self-understanding of the West.
MKD

6   I have discussed this critique at length in my introduction to *On the Pathos of Truth* in this volume. I note in this regard that in his final call to his readers Nietzsche makes one significant change in the revised preface. In the original version, Nietzsche speaks as follows: ". . . you contemplative ones whose eyes do not perhaps grope about with hasty peering at the exterior of things, but know how to find the approach to the kernel of their essence . . ." The revised version reads as follows: "You contemplative ones whose eyes are incapable of gliding with hasty peering from one surface to another." Nietzsche's omission of any reference to "essence" seems consistent with his suggestion in *On the Pathos of Truth* that we do not have access to what is outside or underlies consciousness.

THOUGHTS ON THE FUTURE OF OUR EDUCATIONAL INSTITUTIONS

Preface.

The reader, from whom I expect something, must have three qualities. He must be at rest and read without haste. He must not always be bringing himself and his "education" in between. Finally he should not expect at the conclusion, as a result for instance, tables. Tables and new curricula for Gymnasiums and other schools I do not promise, I marvel much more at the super-powerful nature of those who are in a position to traverse the whole way, from out of the depths of empiricism up to the heights of the genuine problems of culture and again down from there into the lowlands of the driest regulations and of the most elegant works of tables; but I am satisfied, if I, in the midst of gasping, have climbed a passable mountain and permitted myself to delight over the free view, even if in this book I should never be able to satisfy the friends of tables. I daresay I see a time coming in which serious human beings, in the service of a fully renewed and purified culture [Bildung] and in common labor, even again become the legislators of everyday education [Erziehung] – of education [Erziehung] toward just that culture [Bildung]; probably they must then again make tables – but how distant is the time! And what all will not have occurred in between! Perhaps lying between it and the present is the annihilation of the Gymnasium, perhaps even the annihilation of the university, or at least[1] such a total reformation of the so-called educational institutions

1   Here Nietzsche substitutes "wenigstens" for "mindestens" in the earlier

that their old tables might offer themselves to later eyes like remainders out of the time of the lake-dwellings.[2]

The book is designed [bestimmt] for calm readers, for human beings who are still not swept up in the dizzying haste of our rolling age and still do not feel an idolatrous pleasure when they throw themselves under its wheels, thus for human beings who have still not accustomed themselves to estimate the value of everything according to whether it is time-sparing or time-wasting. That means – for few human beings. These "still have time"; these may, without blushing before themselves, seek together the most fruitful and the most powerful moments of their day in order to reflect on the future of our education; these may even believe themselves to have come till evening in a right useful and worthy manner, namely in the *meditatio generis futuri*.[3] Such a human being has still not unlearned how to think while he reads, he still understands how to read the secret between the lines, indeed he is of such a wasteful type that he even still reflects over that which was read – perhaps long after the book itself has left the hands. And indeed not in order to write a review or another book, but only in order to reflect! Light-minded wastrel! You are my reader, for you are calm enough to be able to set out together on a distant way with the author, whose goal he cannot see, in whose goal he must honestly believe, in order that a later, perhaps distant generation should see with its eyes, where we, blind and only led by instinct, grope. If against that the reader should be of the opinion it requires only a swift leap, a cheerful deed, if he for instance considers everything to be achieved with a newly introduced "organization" by the state, thus we must fear that he has understood neither the author nor the authentic problem.

Finally the third and most important demand is handed down to him that he in no case, after the manner of the modern human being, be permitted to bring himself and his education without pause, for instance as a measuring stick, in between as if with that he would possess a criterion of all things. We wish that he may be educated enough

version of the text.

2   Nietzsche refers to the early human settlements consisting of houses on stilts built in or along lakes.

3   Latin for "contemplation of the genus of the future."

in order rightly to think little of his education, indeed to despise it. Then he may with the greatest trust surrender himself to the leading of the author, to whom it is permitted to dare, exactly from not-knowing and from knowledge about not-knowing, to speak to him. Nothing other does he want to claim for himself before others than a strongly excited feeling for the specific character of our German barbarism, for that which so designates us as the barbarians of the nineteenth century in the face of other barbarians. Now he seeks, with this book in hand, after such who will be driven hither and yon by a similar feeling. Let yourselves be found, you isolated ones in whose existence I believe! You selfless ones, who suffer in yourselves the suffering and destruction of the German spirit! You contemplative ones whose eyes are incapable of gliding with hasty peering from one surface to another. You high-minded ones, of whom Aristotle says in praise that you go through life hesitating and deedless, except where a great honor and a great work clamor after you![4] You I call up. Only this time do not crawl away into the cave of your seclusion and your mistrust. Think you this book is determined to be your herald. When you yourself, in your own armor, appear upon the battlefield, who might still crave then to look back at the herald who called you? –

---

4   Here Nietzsche uses Hochsinnigen to refer to Aristotle's μεγαλόψυχος, the great-souled man. See *Nicomachean Ethics*, 1124b24–26.

DIGNITY AND DECAY

We are temporal beings, in motion in both our bodies and our thoughts. We are becoming, and we are mortal. Yet, what we desire perhaps above all else is being, eternal existence without change or motion. What does this desire truly aim at? Whatever the true aim of the desire is, we may suspect and even fear that that desire cannot be fully satisfied. For this, we are in need of consolation. In *The Greek State*, Nietzsche tells us that adequate consolation can be found in a particular kind of politics, which is part of what he calls the "artistic culture." He attributes this solution not to his own genius, but to Plato: it is the "*secret teaching*" of Plato's *Republic*.

Nietzsche turns to the Greek state, which he regards as the paramount example of an artistic culture, apparently after having noted the insufficiency of the modern effort at consolation. He maintains that the modern world's consolation takes the form of two concepts, the "dignity of the human being" and the "dignity of work." Both the human being and work are presented as kinds of motions that belong to the struggle for existence. However, Nietzsche argues that the value of existence, the being at which these motions aim, has not been sufficiently established by the modern world.

Does what we mean by "existence," particularly in phrases like "the struggle for existence," live up to that desired thing that we call being? Is existence eternal and unchanging? If it is not, then what would suggest it has self-evident dignity?

Rather than trying to establish the worth of mere existence, Nietzsche implies that any adequate consolation for human temporality must speak to two needs that attend human life, the need to struggle for existence and the need for art. In the modern effort at consolation the need to struggle for existence is well and openly represented in the contemporary slogans. "Human being" represents existence, and "work" represents struggle. But does the modern effort address the need for art? Perhaps in a muted or hidden way the need for art is represented by the term "dignity." But this is hardly explicit.

Nietzsche seems to trace the absence of an explicit response to this need to the way the modern world creates human beings. According to Nietzsche, it creates human beings that are composed of parts that have been incoherently thrown together. There is apparently no plan or direction to this making. The effect of the incoherence of modern human beings is that the need to struggle to survive and the need for art exist "often at the same time in the same human being." Nietzsche implies that this condition is unintelligible because these needs are by nature arranged hierarchically, with the need for art as the authoritative need. When these needs co-exist in the same human being, an "unnatural melting" together of these two drives occurs, and the order is no longer recognized by the human in whom they exist. What Nietzsche implies by this is that the human being must be ordered if he is to see order in the world. Disorder disrupts vision, and the need for art disappears from view. At best it only manifests itself in muted ways not likely to be recognized.

Nietzsche seems to imply that the absence of a more explicit awareness of the need for art accounts for the inadequacy of the consolation offered by the modern world. By contrast, Nietzsche maintains that, unlike modern human beings, the Ancient Greeks can admit with shocking openness that both the human being and work are disgraceful. They are not crushed by this conclusion; rather, they seem able to withstand it because their culture is ordered with a view to art.

Though he stresses the need for art, Nietzsche does not say explicitly what that means. Perhaps the best way to begin to understand what Nietzsche means by art is to examine what Plutarch says about the Greeks' attitude toward the artist and the artifacts he makes. The particular case that Plutarch uses is that of sculptors and their statues. "Plutarch says once with an ancient Greek instinct, no nobly born youth will have the longing if he looks at the Zeus in Pisa, to become himself a Phidias. . . . Artistic creating falls for the Greeks just so much under the non-respect-worthy concept of work, like every banausic handicraft." This example makes it clear that what is needed in "the need for art" is not some doing or making, not some motion, but the final product, the artifact. What is most crucial, however, is that Nietzsche seems to understand art as the rational account of becoming in terms of the end at which it aims. The becoming is a means to this end. As such, it seems to have no value in itself. By contrast, the end appears to have being. For this reason, it seems, it also has value and dignity.

By moving immediately from the example of the artist to a discussion of reproduction, Nietzsche seems to suggest that the Greeks understand art as an imitation of nature: nature also seems to have motions that aim at ends. The proximate aim of reproduction seems to be the child. According to Nietzsche, the Greek father regards the birthing of the child in the same way he regards the making of an artifact: "[It] appears to him like all becomings in nature, as a violent necessity, as a pressing itself into existence." Though the father averts his eyes from the child's birthing, he treats the child, or more specifically the child's "beauty and talent," as things with being; therefore, he admires them. So too, the Greek admires the statue of Zeus, but he regards Phidias' working as disgraceful.

By associating being with dignity, Nietzsche prompts us to ask what the basis is for this connection. To begin, this association suggests that Nietzsche thinks at least part of the desire for being is the same as or inseparable from the desire for dignity. Dignity is a moral concept. The human being who wants to be dignified tries to act according to universal laws that define what is high and that he regards as authoritative: "I am such and such a person, one who will do actions of this kind, but not actions of that sort." Laws that are universal and defining make the world intelligible for the moral human being, and this intelligibility locates and defines dignity. Now the highest law and therefore the most authoritative law we can imagine seems to be one that is eternal. And this seems to suggest that we regard being as *better, higher* than becoming.

But is there no way to locate dignity, or moral worth, in becoming, or motion? In his treatment of the "dignity of work," Nietzsche denied work its own dignity, because work was instrumental, a mere means in the service of the end of staying alive. It would seem that instrumental things actually locate their worth only in their ends. Can motion ever have worth in itself, or are we fated always to consider motion as a means to an end? To answer this question, it may be helpful to consider how one might evaluate motion. We seem able to speak of the starting and stopping points of motion. We also seem able to compare the motion of a thing to other things. For example, we can speak of a train speeding past a gate. What we really seem to be doing in these examples, however, is thinking of motion as if it is composed of points or a sequence of moments. In other words, we are thinking of it as a series of starts and stops. A gate acts like a point at which the train's motion ceases. But in fact this starting and stopping is not motion; rather, it seems to be a conceptual framework we place upon motion to make it intelligible to us. Motion in itself might not be intelligible. Does our judgment that being is superior to becoming depend upon our sense that motion may not be truly intelligible? This would suggest that dignity, intelligibility, and being are inter-related.

The judgment in favor of being seems to permeate all of our perceptions and all of our thoughts. Passing away offends us, and decay does not seem dignified. We may need consolation for our temporality in part because we love ourselves, and we want what are to persist. But we also need consolation because our temporality seems to us to be an indictment of what we are.

With this, we arrive at what seems to be the crux of Nietzsche's argument. Our desire for being cannot be fully satisfied in our mortal life; however, art, as Nietzsche describes it, offers us a way to understand our becoming in terms of the end at which it aims. Nietzsche implies that this artistic understanding satisfies our desire for dignity and makes us intelligible to ourselves. Thus, there are grounds for restating the desire for being as the need for art. Since the modern world is not ordered with a view to art, it does not offer human beings dignity and intelligibility. It therefore cannot console them.

As an alternative to the politics of the modern world, one might turn to nature. Reproduction also seems to be a natural consolation for our temporality. However, Nietzsche implies that reproduction cannot fulfill the desire for immortality as well as the artistic culture can. Thus, nature may be said to point beyond itself to politics and to the artistic culture in particular. Does this mean the artistic culture is properly understood as natural?

The artistic culture Nietzsche describes is hierarchically ordered in a way that repeats the natural hierarchy of the need to struggle for existence and the need for art. Whereas in the modern world these needs are often melted together in a single human being, in the artistic culture, these needs are allocated to two classes of human beings. Thus, artistic culture replaces the modern emphasis on the absolute individual with an emphasis on the whole that is the state. Nietzsche seems to imply that splitting the two needs between hierarchically ordered classes is the natural way for these drives to co-exist. He also seems to imply that this is the best way to ensure that the need for art is recognized and addressed by human beings. Is this simply because he thinks a human being who is constantly occupied with the need to sustain himself lacks the leisure necessary to become aware of and respond to the need for art? Or does Nietzsche think the struggle for existence has an effect on a human being that renders him unsuitable or even unable to be an artist?

The latter possibility is particularly somber since the need to struggle for existence is actually increased for the slave class that bears this burden. The slaves must provide for their own needs as well as for the needs of those in the "more favored" upper class. Those in the more favored class are "whisked away from the struggle for existence in order . . . to produce and to satisfy" the need for art, which Nietzsche characterizes as "a new world of requirements."

The particular artifact, if it may be so called, at which the artistic culture aims is the genius. One may wonder how the genius is supposed to answer our desire for immortality better than the child. As the beginning of an answer, we may note that when Nietzsche speaks of the genius, he does not seem to refer to the individual in whom genius manifests itself but to the quality of genius. The quality of genius cannot include idiosyncratic characteristics; rather, it must be defined by universal concepts. This universality seems necessary if the genius is to be recognized as such for all time and if we are to believe that the manifestation of genius will always be a possibility in the future.

The recurrence of the genius throughout history does not seem to be a sufficient answer to the question of why the genius satisfies our longing for immortality better than a child might. We may recall that Nietzsche says the father admires the beauty and talent of his child. These attributes seem comparable to genius in their generality. Despite this, Nietzsche implies that they are less adequate than genius. Is the difference between the genius and the child's attributes quantitative? Does the genius have more beauty and talent than the child? It seems likely that this is at least part of Nietzsche's view. Is there also a qualitative difference? Nietzsche seems to understand the genius as a kind of world-maker. In *On the Pathos of Truth*, Nietzsche describes the genius Heraclitus as someone who stood like an unmoved mover amid a solar system. Do we revolve around the genius like planets around a life-giving god or sun?

According to Nietzsche, the genius confers dignity upon all who consciously or unconsciously contribute to his making. The individual in whom genius is manifest is not exempt from this claim. This individual too is only dignified to the extent that he contributes to the creation of another genius. As Nietzsche describes him, the genius fulfills our moral sense and acts as a kind of anchor for our moral actions. The genius is the natural end at which Nietzsche implies every human being aims, unconsciously or consciously.

Nietzsche associates the artistic culture and the genius with nature, which we tend to equate with truth. However, he often seems to slide seamlessly from talk of nature to talk of illusion. Is the consolation he claims is afforded by the artistic culture true or illusory? Does the end of genius at which our becoming aims reveal intelligibility to us, or does it help us to impose a structure on the world that makes the world intelligible to us? Nietzsche admits that the artistic culture depends upon at least a partial obscuring of truth. He tells us that shame, the awareness of oneself as a means to a higher end, is the concept that orders the artistic culture. He also tells us that in the feeling of shame "the unconscious knowledge" that the artistic culture depends for its existence on the horror of slavery "hides from itself." To illustrate both the beauty and the horror of the artistic culture, Nietzsche offers us the second mythic creature to appear in the essay, the sphinx: "in that requirement [for work and slavery] lies the horrible and the bestial of the Sphinx nature, which in the glorification of the artistic, free life of culture stretches forth such a beautiful young woman's body." The beauty of the artistic culture is what presents itself to us initially, and perhaps it is all that most human beings in the artistic culture ever see with any clarity. However, if one looks past the beauty, one sees its terrifying origins. Furthermore, one sees that beauty and the terrible are parts of the same whole.

By using the image of the sphinx, does Nietzsche allude to the sphinx that posed the riddle to Oedipus? The sphinx asks what has one voice but walks on four legs in the morning, two legs at noon, and three legs in the evening. Oedipus answers that this temporal being is the human being. If Nietzsche does mean to allude to this sphinx, what are we to make of the fact that Oedipus's correct answer brings tragedy to himself and his city and causes him to blind himself? Does this mean that neither the human being nor the artistic culture can endure complete clarity about our temporality? Do we therefore *require* illusions?

Finally, we may wonder whether and how Nietzsche intends the sphinx to be contrasted with the image of the centaur, which he used to represent the incoherence of modern human beings. Like the centaur, the sphinx is part human and part beast. Unlike the centaur, Nietzsche does not suggest that the sphinx is incoherent. Rather, the sphinx's parts and their order seem to correspond to Nietzsche's understanding of the human being. The lion might represent the ferocity and motion that Nietzsche thinks underlies and supports order and rest, those aspects of a human being that we want to claim as human in contradistinction to the underlying motion. We might wish to relegate this motion to beasts and to nature rather than admitting that it may be part of what we are. Do the wings represent the human desire to transcend becoming?

If the artistic culture corresponds with human nature as it presents itself to us, does this mean it also corresponds with nature simply? Nietzsche seems to insist that we can see that nature corresponds to what the sphinx represents. This truth falls into our eyes as "organs in accord with the world and the earth":

> Whatever wants to live, that is must live, in this terrible
> constellation of things, is at the bottom of its essence a portrait of the original pain and of the original contradiction,

thus must fall into our eyes as "organs in accord with the world and the earth," as insatiable lust for existence and eternal self-contradiction in the form of time, thus as *becoming*. Every moment devours the one that went before, every birth is the death of countless beings; begetting, living, and murdering is one.

If we look more closely at this assertion, however, we find that Nietzsche, through Goethe's *Faust*, attributes this claim to an angel, Pater Seraphicus. This father angel has the ability to see the world from both a human perspective and a divine perspective. This ability seems to put him in a position to verify that the world is as we experience it. But we cannot step outside the human perspective, and so we cannot verify for ourselves the truth of the angel's claim. We cannot know whether what we hold true accords with the truth that may be seen from a supra-human, transcendent perspective, and we may even lack the ability to tell whether there is any such transcendent truth outside the limits of our own organs. This may be the problem Nietzsche tries to represent when he mixes the language of nature with illusion. He seems to grant that we distinguish between these things and that these distinctions are meaningful for human beings; however, he may also wonder what the ultimate status of these distinctions is. Perhaps he thinks we are unable to answer this question in the absence of divine intervention.

LvB

THE GREEK STATE

Preface.

We moderns[1] have an advantage over the Greeks in two concepts, which as it were have been given as a means of consolation to a world comporting itself slavishly throughout and at the same time anxiously shying away from the word "slave": we speak of the dignity [Würde] of the human being and of the "dignity of work." Everything tortures itself, in order miserably to perpetuate a miserable life; this fearful necessity compels toward consuming work, which now the human being seduced by the "will" – or more correctly – human intellect casually [gelegentlich] stares at as something full of dignity. But so that work has a pretension to an honoring title, it would indeed be necessary before everything that existence itself, for which it is indeed only a tortuous means, have somewhat more dignity and value than this has manifested [erschienen] up till now to seriously intended philosophies and religions. What else may we find in the necessity to work of all the millions than the drive to exist at any price, the same all-powerful drive by which stunted plants stretch their roots into soilless stone!

Out of this dreadful struggle-for-existence can pop up only the individuals who now immediately again will be preoccupied by the noble, illusory images of an artistic culture [Kultur], so that they do not only come to the practical pessimism that nature abhors as the true unnature. In the modern[2] world which, considered[3] together with the

1 More literally, "newer ones."
2 More literally, "newer."

Greek one, at most only creates abnormalities and centaurs, in which the individual human being, like that fabulous being at the opening of Horace's Poetics,[4] is colorfully put together out of pieces, the lust of the struggle-for-existence and the need for art shows itself often at the same time in the same human being: out of which unnatural melting together the necessity has emerged to excuse and to consecrate that first lust before the need for art. Therefore one believes in the "dignity of the human being" and the "dignity of work."

The Greeks do not need such conceptual-hallucinations; with them it is expressed with shocking openness that work is a disgrace – and a secret and seldom speaking but generally living wisdom adds also that the human thing is a disgraceful and lamentable nothing and a "shadow dream."[5] Work is a disgrace because existence shines forth in the seducing adornment of artistic illusions and now really appears to have a value in itself, thus holds even then still that principle that work is a disgrace – and indeed in the feeling of the impossibility that the human being struggling for the sake of naked survival could be an *artist*. In modern times,[6] not the human being, in need of art, rather the slave determines the general ideas: as such, according to his nature, [he]

3   More literally, "held."
4   Quintus Horatius Flaccus, *De Arte Poetica*, 1–5: Humano capiti cervicem picter equinam iungere si velit, et varias iuducere plumas undique collatis membris, ut turpiter atrum desinat in piscem mulier Formosa superne, spectatum admissi risum teneatis, amici? "If a painter chose to join a human head to the neck of a horse, and to spread feathers of many a hue over limbs picked up now here now there, so that what at the top is a lovely woman ends below in a black and ugly fish, could you, my friends, if favored with a private view, refrain from laughing?" H. Rushton Fairclugh, translator; New York: G. P. Putnam's Sons, 1932.
5   Pindar, *Pythian Odes*, VIII, 92–96: ἐν δ' ὀλίγωι βροτῶν τὸ τερπνὸν αὔξεται· οὕτω δὲ καὶ πιτνεῖ χαμαί, ἀποτρόπωι γνώμαι σεσεισμένον. ἐπάμεροι· τί δέ τις; τί δ' οὔ τις; σκιᾶς ὄναρ ἄνθρωπος. "Short is the space of time in which the happiness of mortal men groweth up, and even so, doth it fall to the ground, when stricken down by adverse doom. Creatures of a day, what is any one? What is he not? Man is but a dream of a shadow." Sir John Sandys, translator; Cambridge: Harvard University Press, 1937.
6   More literally, "the newer time."

must designate all his circumstances[7] with deceptive names in order to be able to live. Such phantoms, as the dignity of the human being, the dignity of work, are the needy products of a slavish condition hiding from itself. Unblessed time, in which the slave needs such concepts, in which he is stirred up to reflection on himself and out above himself [über sich und über sich hinaus]! Unblessed seducer who has annihilated the innocent position of the slave through the fruit of the tree of knowledge! Now this one must hold out with such transparent lies from one day to the other as they are recognizable for anyone looking more deeply into the alleged "equal rights of all" or into the so-called "basic rights of the human being," of the human being as such, or into the dignity of work. Indeed he is not permitted to conceive upon what level and in what height "dignity," first, roughly can be spoken of, namely there where the individual fully surpasses himself and no longer must produce[8] and work in the service of his individual continued living.

And even upon this height of "work" a feeling occasionally comes over the Greeks that looks like shame. Plutarch says once[9] with an ancient Greek instinct, no nobly born youth will have the longing if he looks at the Zeus in Pisa, to become himself a Phidias,[10] or if he sees the Hera in Argos to become himself a Polyklet:[11] and just as little

7 Or "relations."
8 Or "procreate."
9 Plutarch, *Life of Pericles*, Ch. 2: "Labor with one's own hands on lowly tasks gives witness, in the toil thus expended on useless things, to one's own indifference to higher things. No generous youth, from seeing the Zeus at Pisa, or the Hera at Argos, longs to be Pheidias or Polycleitus; nor to be Anacreon or Philetas or Archilochus out of pleasure in their poems. For it does not of necessity follow that, if the work delights you with its grace, the one who wrought it is worthy of your esteem. Wherefore the spectator is not advantaged by those things at the sight of which no ardor for imitation [μιμητικός] arises in the breast, nor any uplift of the soul arousing zealous [ζῆλος] impulses to do the like." G. P. Putnam's Sons, 1916.
10 Phidias (c. 465–425 B.C.) was an Athenian sculptor regarded as the greatest and most versatile among the Greeks. His statue of Zeus was over twelve meters tall and depicted Zeus on a highly embellished throne, holding victory in one hand and a scepter in the other.

would he wish to be Anacreon, Philetas, or Archilochus,[12] however much he even delights[13] in their poetries. Artistic creating falls for the Greeks just so much under the non-respect-worthy concept of work, like every banausic[14] handicraft. But if the compelling force of the artistic drive works in him, then he *must* create and subject himself to that necessity of work. And as a father admires the beauty and talent of his child, but thinks of the act of his birth [Entstehung] with shameful aversion, thus it goes with the Greek. The delightful marveling [Staunen] at the beautiful has not blinded him about its becoming – that appears to him like all becoming in nature, as a violent necessity, as a pressing itself into existence. The same feeling, with which the process of procreation[15] is considered as something shameful to be hidden, although in it the human being serves a higher goal than his individual preservation: the same feeling fogs up around [umschleierte] even the birth [Entstehung] of the great work of art, despite the fact that through it a higher form of existence is inaugurated, as through that act a new generation is. *Shame* appears consequently to enter in there where the human being is still only a tool of unendingly greater appearances of will than he may value [gelten] himself in the singular form of the individual.

Now we have the general concept under which the feelings that the Greeks had in regard to work and to slavery are to be ordered. They held both as a necessary disgrace, in the face of which one feels *shame*, at the same time disgrace, at the same time necessity. In this feeling of shame the unconscious knowledge hides from itself that the authentic goal *requires* these presuppositions, but that in that *requirement* lies the horrible [Entsetztliche] and the bestial of the Sphinx nature, which in

11 Polyklet (c. 460–410 B.C.) was an Argive sculptor renowned especially for his depictions of mortals. All of his statues were of bronze except for the Hera in Argos, which was of chryselephantine.
12 Anacreon was a lyric poet (c. 575–490 B.C.); Philetas (born c. 340 B.C.) was a poet and scholar; Archilochus was one of the earliest Ionian lyric poets (c. seventh century B.C.); little survives of any of their works.
13 Reading "ergötzen" for "ergetzen."
14 Banausic is an adjective derived from the Greek βαναυσικός, referring to the practices of the types of manual or mechanical arts that destroy the body and degrade the soul. See Xenophon, *Oeconomicus*, IV.2 and VI.5.

the glorification of the artistic, free life of culture [Kulturleben] stretches forth such a beautiful young woman's body. Culture [Bildung], which is nobly the true requirement of art, rests upon a terrifying [erschrecklichen] ground: but this gives itself to be recognized in the dawning [dämmernde] feeling of shame. So that there is a broad, deep, and fertile soil [Erdboden] for the development of art, the monstrous majority, in the service of a minority, must be slavishly subjected to life's necessities *above* and beyond their individual requirements.[16] At its expense, through its working more, that favored class is supposed to be whisked away from the struggle for existence, in order now to produce and to satisfy a new world of requirements.

According to this we must therefore understand, as a cruel-sounding truth to be put down, that *slavery belongs to the essence of a culture* [Kultur]: a truth, of course, which leaves over no doubt about the absolute worth[17] of existence. *This truth* is the vulture that gnaws upon the liver of the Promethean promoter of culture. The misery of the human being living with difficulty must still be increased, in order to make possible the production of a world of art for a small number of Olympian human beings. Here lies the source of that wrath, which the communists and socialists and also their paler derivatives, the white race of "liberals" of every time, have nurtured against the arts, but also against classical antiquity. If culture [Kultur] really were granted to the discretion of a people, if inescapable powers did not rule here, which are law and limit to the individual, thus the contempt [Verachtung] of culture [Kultur], the glorification of poverty of spirit, the iconoclastic annihilation of artistic claims would be more than the revolt of the downtrodden [unterdrückten] masses against the dronelike individuals: it would be the cry of pity, which pulls down the walls of culture [Kultur]; the drive after equity, after an equal measure of suffering, would overflow into all other ideas. Really an excessive degree of pity has at times for a short while, here and there, broken through all the dams of the cultural life [Kulturlebens]; a rainbow of pitying love and of peace appeared with the first shimmering of Christendom, and under it was born its most beautiful fruit, the evangel of John. But there

16 Or "needs."
17 Or "value."

are also examples that powerful [mächtige] religions petrify a certain degree of culture [Kulturgrad] over long periods of time and cut down with a pitiless[18] sickle everything that wants further to grow still more strong [kräftig]. One, namely, is not to be forgotten: this same cruelty, which we find in the essence of every culture [Kultur], lies also in the essence of every powerful [mächtige] religion and generally in the nature of *power* [Macht], which is always evil; so that we will understand it well just as much if a culture [Kultur] with a cry for freedom or at least equity breaks down an all-too-high-towering bulwark of religious claims. Whatever wants to live, that is, must live, in this terrible constellation of things, is at the bottom [Grunde] of its essence a portrait of the original pain [Urschmerzes] and of the original contradiction [Urwiderspruches], thus must fall into our eyes as "organs in accord with the world and the earth,"[19] as insatiable lust for existence and eternal self-contradiction in the form of time, thus as *becoming*. Every moment devours [frißt][20] the one that went before, every birth is the death of countless beings; begetting, living, and murdering is one. Therefore we may even compare the glorious[21] culture with a victor dripping with blood, who in his triumphal procession drags along the conquered ones chained to his wagon as slaves: at which a charitable power has blinded their eyes, so that they, almost crushed by the wheels of the wagon, yet still call out "the dignity of work!" "the dignity of the human being!" The luxurious Cleopatra culture [Kultur] ever casts inestimable pearls into her golden cup: these pearls are the tears of pity for the slave and for the misery of the slave. Out of the softening of the modern[22] human being are born the conditions of monstrous social need of the present, not out of true and deep compassion with that misery; and if it should be true that the Greeks perished from their slavery, thus this other thing is much more certain, that we will perish from the *lack* of slavery: which neither original Christendom nor Germandom thought in any way objectionable, to say nothing of

18 Or "inexorable."
19 *Faust* II, line 11906.
20 Freßen is a verb specially designated for the way in which animals eat.
21 More literally, "lordly."
22 More literally, "newer."

being reprehensible. How sublimely does the consideration of the medieval serf work upon us, with the internally strong and tender relations of right and of morals ordered toward the higher one, with the profound [tiefsinnig] enclosure of his narrow existence – how sublime – and how reproachful!

Whoever now cannot reflect about the configuration of society without melancholy, whoever has learned to conceive of it as the ongoing painful birth of those eximious[23] human beings of culture [Kulturmenschen], in whose service everything else must consume itself, that one will also no longer be deceived by that false glitter which the moderns[24] have spread over the origin and the significance of the state. Namely, what can the state signify to us if it is not the means with which to bring into motion that previously sketched social process and to guarantee it in its unhindered continuance. The drive toward sociability in individual human beings may even still be so strong, [but] first the iron clasp of the state presses the great masses so into one another that now that chemical division of society, with its new, pyramidal arrangement, *must* advance. But from where springs forth this sudden power [Macht] of the state, whose goal lies far forward above the discernment[25] and above the egoism of the individual? How did the slave *emerge*, the blind mole of culture [Kultur]? The Greeks revealed it to us in their instincts regarding the relations of right between peoples, who, even in the ripest fullness of their civilization and humanity, did not cease to cry out from a mouth of metal [erzenem] such words as "to the victor belongs the defeated,[26] with woman and child, goods and blood. Force[27] gives the first *right*, and there is no right that is not in its foundation arrogance, usurpation, act of force."[28]

Here we see again with what pitiless rigidity nature, in order to come to society, forged that cruel tool, the state – namely those *conquerors* with the iron hand that are nothing other than the objectifica-

---

23 A rare word derived from Latin, meaning excellent or distinguished.
24 More literally, "newer ones."
25 More literally, "insight."
26 Or "victim."
27 Or "violence."
28 Or "act of violence."

tion of that designated instinct. In the indefinable greatness and power [Macht] of such conquerors, the observer [Betrachter] scents [spurt] that they are only a means for an intention revealing itself in them and yet concealing itself from them. It is just as though a magic [magischer] will went out from them, so puzzlingly swiftly do the weaker powers [Kräfte] attach themselves to them, so wonderfully do they transform themselves, at the sudden swelling of that avalanche of force,[29] under the magic [Zauber] of that creative kernel, into an affinity up till now not present therein.

If we now see, forthwith, how little the downtrodden ones concerned themselves about the dreadful origin of the state, so that at bottom about no kind of event does history report worse to us than about the coming into being of the state of affairs of these sudden, violent [gewaltsamen], bloody, and at least in *one* point inexplicable usurpations: much more, if hearts involuntarily swell toward the magic [Magie] of the becoming state, with the presentiment of an invisible deep intention, there where the calculating understanding is capable of seeing only an addition of powers [Kräfte]: if now, what is more, the state is considered [betrachtet] with ardor as the goal and peak of the sacrifices[30] and duties of the individual: thus all this expresses the monstrous necessity of the state, without which nature should not succeed to come through society to its redemption in appearance, in the mirror of the genius. What kind of knowledge does the instinctive pleasure in the state not overcome! One should indeed think that a being that looks into the emergence of the state, in the future would seek his salvation [Heil] only at a shuddersome distance from it; and where can one not see the memorials of its emergence, wasted lands, destroyed cities, human beings become wild, consuming hatred of peoples! The state, of disgraceful birth, for most human beings a continually flowing fountain[31] of hardship, in frequently recurring periods the devouring torch of the human race – and nevertheless a sound, at which we forget ourselves, a call to battle that has inspired to countless truly heroic deeds, perhaps the highest object and most worthy of

29 Or "violence."
30 More literally, "offerings."
31 Or "source."

respect for the blind and egoistic mass, which also has the strange expression of greatness upon its face only in the monstrous moments in the life of the state!

But we have to construe the Greeks, with a view to the singular solar altitude of their art, already a priori[32] as the "political human beings as such"; and really history knows no second example of such a fearsome unchaining of the political drive, of such an unconditional sacrifice [Hinopferung] of all other interests in the service of this instinct for the state – at best [höchstens] one could in a comparative manner and from similar grounds honor [auszeichnen] the human beings of the Renaissance in Italy with a similar title. That drive is so overcharged with the Greeks that it begins ever again afresh [von Neuem] to rage against itself and sink its teeth into its own flesh. This bloody jealousy of city toward city, of party toward party, this murderous lust of those small wars, the tigerish triumph over the corpse of the killed enemy, in short the incessant renewal of those Trojan scenes of war and atrocity, into which spectacle Homer stands before us fully, *pleasurably* immersed, as a genuine Hellene – to where does this naïve barbarity of the Greek state point, from where does it take its excuse before the tribunal[33] of eternal justice?[34] Proudly and calmly the state stands before it: and it leads by the hand the gloriously blooming woman, Greek society. For this Helen it conducted those wars – what grey-bearded judge could condemn here?[35]

With this mysterious [geheimnißvoll] connection that we divine here between the state and art, political lust and artistic procreation, battlefield and art work, we understand by the state, as has been said, only the iron clasp that compels the social process: whereas without the state, in a natural bellum omnium contra omnes,[36] society general-

32 Latin for "from what is before."
33 More literally, "judge's seat."
34 Gerechigkeit is translated elsewhere as "equity."
35 An allusion to *Iliad*, Book III, lines 156–157, where the elders of the people [δημογέροντες] say of Helen: οὐ νέμεσις Τρῶας καὶ ἐυκνήμιδας Ἀχαιοὺς τοιῆδ' ἀμφὶ γυναικὶ πολὺν χρόνον ἄλγεα πάσχειν. "No blame that both the Trojans and well-greaved Acheans should for such a woman suffer pain for a long time."
36 Latin for "war of all against all"; this is likely an allusion to Thomas Hobbes's description of the condition faced by human beings living out-

ly cannot take root in a greater measure and out beyond the domain of the family. Now, after the universally entered-into formation of states, that drive of the bellum omnium contra omnes concentrates itself from time to time into horrifying war clouds [made] of peoples and discharges itself, as it were, in rarer but so much stronger blows and streams of weather. But, in the pauses in between, society is yet allowed the time within which, according to the inwardly turned, pressed-together effect of that bellum, to germinate and to turn green all regions, in order to allow, as soon as there are a few warm days, the shining blooms of the genius to sprout forth.

In the face of the political world of the Hellenes I do not want to conceal in which appearances of the present I believe I recognize dangerous atrophies of the political sphere, equally precarious for art and society. If there should be human beings, which by birth, as it were, were placed outside of the instincts of peoples and states, which thus had to allow the state to be valid only so far as they conceived it to be in their own interests: thus will human beings of such a kind necessarily represent to themselves as the final goal of the state the greatest possible undisturbed living next to one another of great political communities, in which *they* before all would be allowed to pursue their own intentions without limitation. With this representation in the head, they will promote the politics that offers these intentions the greatest security, whereas it is unthinkable that they, against their intentions, perhaps led by an unconscious instinct, should bring themselves to a sacrifice for the tendency of the state, unthinkable because they lack just that instinct. All other citizens of the state are, regarding what nature intends for them with their instincts for the state, in the dark and follow blindly; only those standing outside of this instinct know what they want from the state and what the state is supposed to guarantee

side of civil society. In *De Cive*, Book I, paragraph 12, Hobbes uses the phrase "bellum omnium in omnes." In *Philosophical Rudiments concerning Government and Society*, Ch. 1, paragraph 13, he uses the phrase "war of all against all." In the English edition of the *Leviathan*, Part I, Ch. 13, he writes, "during the time men live without a common power to keep them all in awe, they are in that condition which is called war; and such a war, as is of every man, against every man." In the Latin *Leviathan*, Part I, Ch. 13 Hobbes uses the phrase "bello omnium contra omnes."

them. Therefore it is precisely inevitable that such human beings gain a great influence over the state, because they are allowed to consider [betrachten] it as a *means*, whereas all others are, under the power [Macht] of the unconscious intentions of the state, themselves only means for the purposes of the state. In order now, through the means of the state, to reach the highest furtherance of their goals, useful to themselves, before everything it is necessary that the state will be completely freed from those terrible, incalculable convulsions of war, with that it can be used rationally; and with that they strive, as consciously as possible, for a state of affairs in which war is an impossibility. On this score, it is now held as valuable to curtail and to weaken as much as possible the special political drive and through the manufacture of great state bodies of *similar weight* and reciprocal guarantees of security [Sicherstellung] by the same to make the favorable result of an offensive war, and with that war generally, improbable in the highest degree: while they on the other hand[37] seek to wrest the question of war and peace away from the decision of individual possessors of power [Machthaber], in order to be able to appeal much more to the egoism of the mass or its representatives: whereto they in turn have the need slowly to dissolve the monarchic instincts of the people. They correspond to this purpose through the most universal diffusion of the liberal-optimistic consideration of the world, which has its roots in the teaching of the French Enlightenment and Revolution, i.e., in a wholly un-Germanic, genuinely Romanic, superficial[38] and unmetaphysical philosophy. I cannot help seeing before everything the effects of *fear of war* in the presently ruling movement of nationalities and the simultaneous diffusion of the universal right to vote; indeed in the background of these movements, as the genuinely fearing ones, I spot those truly international, homeless financial hermits, who, with their natural lack of instinct for the state, have learned to misuse politics as a means of exchange and the state and society as an apparatus for their own enrichment. Against the diversion, to-be-feared on this side, of the tendency of the state toward the tendency of money the single counter-means is war and war again: in whose excitation at least, still so much

37 More literally, "on the other side."
38 Or "flat."

becomes clear, that the state was not founded upon the fear of the demon of war as the institution of protection of the egoistic individual, rather in the love of the fatherland and of princes it produces out of itself an ethical impulse [Schwung] that refers to a much higher determination. If I thus designate as a dangerous characteristic of the political present the employment of thoughts of revolution in the service of a self-seeking [eigensüchtigen], stateless aristocracy of money, if I conceive the monstrous diffusion of liberal optimism at the same time as the result of the modern [modernen] money economy fallen into peculiar hands and see all the evils [Übel] of the social conditions [Zustände], including the necessary decline [Verfall] of the arts, either germinating out of that root or grown together with it: thus one will have to consider it good for me to occasionally strike up a paean to war. His silver bow resounds fearsomely: and if he comes at once here like the night, thus he is yet Apollo, the just [rechte][39] god of the consecration [Weihe] and purification of the state. But first, as it says in the beginning of the *Iliad*, he speeds the arrow at the mules and dogs. Then he even strikes human beings, and all over the woodpiles blaze with corpses.[40] So let it then be expressed that war is just such a necessity for the state, as the slave [is] for society: and who would be able to withhold[41] these findings[42] from himself, if he asks himself honestly about the grounds of the unreached perfection[43] of Greek art?

39 Or "proper."
40 See *Iliad*, Book I, lines 43–52. In response to the prayer of Chryses, Homer writes: "So he spoke in prayer, and Phoibus Apollo heard him and strode down along the pinnacles of Olympus, angered in his heart, carrying across his shoulders the bow and hooded quiver; and the shafts clashed on the shoulders of the god, walking angrily. He came as night comes down and knelt then apart and opposite from the ships and let go an arrow. Terrible [δεινή] was the clash that rose from the bow of silver. First he went after the mules and the circling hounds, then let go a tearing arrow against the men themselves and struck them. The corpse fires burned everywhere and did not stop burning." Richmond Lattimore translator; Chicago: The University of Chicago Press, 1951.
41 More literally, "withdraw."
42 More literally, "knowledges."
43 Or "completion."

Whoever considers [betrachtet] war and its uniformed potentiality, the *soldier class*, with reference to the essence of the state portrayed so far, must come to the insight, that through war and in the soldier class a copy [Abbild], or perhaps the *original form* [Urbild], *of the state* is placed before our eyes. Here we see, as a universal effect of the tendency of war, an immediate division and partition of the chaotic masses into *military castes*, from which in pyramidal form, upon a broadest of all, slavish, lowliest stratum, the edifice of a "warlike society" raises itself up. The unconscious purpose of the whole movement compels each individual under its yoke and produces[44] even in heterogeneous natures an almost chemical transformation of their properties, until they are brought into an affinity with that purpose. In the higher castes one scents already something more, about which it concerns itself at bottom with this inner process, namely the production[45] of the *military genius* – whom we have learned to recognize as the original founder of states. In many states, e.g., in Sparta's Lycurgan constitution,[46] one can clearly perceive the stamp of that fundamental idea of the state, the production of the military genius. Let us think now the original military state [Urstaat] in the most animated activity, in its authentic "work,"[47] and let us lead the whole practice [Technik][48] of war before our eyes; thus can we not break ourselves free to correct our concepts absorbed from all over, of the "dignity of the human being" and of the "dignity of work" by means of the question, whether the concept of dignity belongs[49] even then to the work which has as its purpose the annihilation [Vernichtung] of "dignified" human beings, whether the concept of dignity applies even to the human being who is entrusted with that "dignified work," or if not, whether, in this warlike task of the state, those concepts, as full of contradictions among one another, do not reciprocally negate [aufheben] each other. I would have thought the warlike human being was a *means* of the military genius and his

44 Or "procreates."
45 Or "procreation."
46 See Plutarch's *Life of Lycurgus*, paragraph 24: "No one was permitted to live as he chose, but all lived in the city as in a soldier's camp."
47 Or "task."
48 Or "technology."
49 More literally, "harmonizes."

work, again, only a means of the same genius; and a degree of dignity comes to him not as an absolute human being and a non-genius; rather to him as a means of the genius – who can even choose his annihilation as a means of the warlike work of art – that dignity namely, *to be considered worthy*[50] *to be the means of genius.* But what has been shown here in one singular example, holds in the most universal sense: every human being, with his collected activity, has only so much dignity, as he, consciously or unconsciously, is a tool of the genius; from which the ethical consequence is immediately to be disclosed that the "human being in itself," the absolute human being, possesses neither dignity, nor rights, nor duties: only as a fully determined being serving unconscious purposes can a human being excuse his existence.

Plato's perfect[51] state is, according to these considerations [Betrachtungen], certainly still something greater than even the warm-blooded among its admirers[52] believe, not to speak at all of the smiling miens of superiority with which our "historically" educated know how to disapprove of such a fruit of antiquity. The authentic goal of the state, the Olympian existence and ever-renewed generation [Zeugung] and preparation of the genius, over against which all others are only tools, means of assistance and enablers, is found here through a poetic intuition and painted with bluntness.[53] Plato thoroughly saw through the terribly ravaged Herm[54] of the life of the state at that time and dis-

---

50 Gewürdigt is related to Würde, which has been translated throughout as "dignity."
51 Or "complete."
52 Or "reverencers."
53 Or "coarseness."
54 Nietzsche refers to a specific incident involving Alcibiades that is described by Thucydides in his *Peloponnesian War*, Book VI, paragraphs 27–28: "In the midst of these preparations all the stone Hermae in the city of Athens, that is to say the customary square figures so common in the doorways of private houses and temples, had in one night most of them their faces mutilated. No one knew who had done it, but large public rewards were offered to find those responsible; and it was further voted that anyone who knew of any other act of impiety having been committed should come and give information without fear of consequences, whether he were citizen, alien, or slave. The matter was taken up the more seriously, as it was thought to be ominous for the expedition, and

cerned even then still something divine in its inside.[55] He believed therein, that one could pull out this divine image and that the grim and barbaric distorted outside did not belong to the essence of the state: the whole ardor and sublimity of his political passion threw itself upon that

> part of a conspiracy to bring about a revolution and to upset the democracy.
>
> Information was accordingly given by some resident aliens and body servants, not about the Hermae but of some previous mutilations of other images perpetrated by young men in a drunken frolic, and of mock celebrations of the Mysteries, alleged to have taken place in private houses. When Alcibiades was implicated in this charge, it was taken up by those who could least endure him, because he stood in the way of their obtaining the undisturbed leadership of The People, and who thought that if he were once removed the first place would be theirs. These accordingly magnified the matter and loudly proclaimed that the affair of the Mysteries and the mutilation of the Hermae were part and parcel of a scheme to overthrow the democracy, and that nothing of all this had been done without Alcibiades; the proofs alledged being the general and undemocratic license of his life and habits." (Richard Crawley translator, slightly revised by Robert B. Strassler, in *The Landmark Thucydides*, New York: The Free Press, 1996).

55 This appears to be yet another allusion to Alcibiades, this time to Alcibiades's speech in Plato's *Symposium*, 221d1–222a6. The connection may be more than casual as the scene involves drunkenness and may be the source of the claim that Alcibiades performed the mysteries in private houses. Alcibiades claims that Socrates resembles Sileni and satyrs both in himself and in his speeches, and says, "his speeches are most like the silenuses when opened up. For were one willing to hear Socrates' speeches, they would at first look altogether laughable. The words and phrases that they wrap around themselves on the outside are like that, the very hide of a hybristic satyr. For he talks of pack-asses, blacksmiths, shoemakers, and tanners, and it looks as if he is always saying the same things through the same things; and hence every inexperienced and foolish human being would laugh at his speeches. But if one sees them opened up and gets oneself inside them, one will find, first, that they alone of speeches have sense inside; and, second, that they are most divine and have the largest number of images of virtue in them; and that they apply to the largest area, indeed to the whole area that it is proper to examine for one who is going to be beautiful and good." (Seth Benardete translator, Chicago: The University of Chicago Press, 2001).

belief, upon that wish – in this glowing fire he burned up. That, in his perfect state, he did not place the genius in his universal concept at the peak, rather only the genius of wisdom and of knowing, that he, however, generally shut out the ingenious artist out of his state, that was a rigid consequence of the Socratic judgment about art[56] which Plato, in a struggle against himself, had made into his own. This more external and nearly accidental omission may not hinder us in recognizing in the total conception of the Platonic state the wonderfully great hieroglyph of a profound [tiefsinnigen] and eternally-to-be interpreted *secret teaching of the connection between the state and the genius*: what we think we have divined of this secret writing, we have said in this preface.

---

56 See Republic 595a; cf. *Republic*, 377b ff.

THE LIVING AND THE ETERNAL

In *The Relation of Schopenhauerian Philosophy to a German Culture*, the title characters, German Culture and Schopenhauer (or his philosophy), hardly appear. One could perhaps argue they do not appear at all.

Throughout this preface the reader finds something that is called, or perhaps calls itself, "German Culture," but much of the text seems to point to the conclusion that while that something may be German, it is not a culture. What, then, does it take for something to be a culture? How is it possible to be a people and not to have a culture? As Nietzsche expresses it in *On the Pathos of Truth*, the fundamental thought of culture is that "the great moments form a chain, that they, like a mountain range, bind humanity through the millennia." This is the idea of *culture*, not of *a* culture or of a *German* culture. Culture here depends upon greatness, upon human greatness, upon geniuses linked one to the other. And not only that. The greatness must be a living greatness, that means it must be in some way capable of participation, maybe even repetition; it must not be time bound, such "that for me the greatness of a past time is also great" (*On the Pathos of Truth*, para. 2).

In the "lowly," contemporary Germany that Nietzsche describes, greatness is met by the "envious looks" of those who "make themselves heavy like lead" and try to drag everything great down to their level, "shamelessly." Envy, while it may recognize greatness as a kind of hated difference, does not wish to recognize greatness as great. The two classes to whom Nietzsche devotes the most attention in this preface, the Philistines and the so-called "cultured" class, both seem possessed by envy, in that they have leading characteristics, complacency on the one hand and historical education on the other, seemingly designed to save them from the sublime or the elevated. But in this Germany, there is also a "general tumult" that may constitute an even more significant challenge to culture. This tumult is caused by those "running toward 'happiness.'" Happiness, especially if it is understood to mean nothing but pleasure, is the goal most narrowly bound to the here and now, to the "present day" and to the "current;" the pursuit of pleasure is most directed away from the eternal.

How then can what holds sway in such a Germany be a culture? How can it perform the role of a culture, which Nietzsche implies at the end of the preface is to be serious and creative, to redeem the German spirit, to purify German virtues? What is to be done when one finds oneself in a place that has no culture? In response to such an urgent question, perhaps the thought occurs to seek that upon which any culture was said to depend, great human beings, geniuses.

And here at the end, after recommending a series of questions to all the Germans designed to expose their lack of culture, Nietzsche introduces the presence of a genius of wisdom, a philosopher, Arthur Schopenhauer. Schopenhauer is presented as the single, German philosopher of the century and perhaps the solution to the German dilemma. "Here you have the philosopher – now seek the culture belonging to him!" The suggestion seems to be that there is a culture that corresponds to a philosopher and that a philosopher is one around whom a culture might be built.

What is most immediately remarkable about this suggestion is the manner in which it seems to reverse the apparent concerns of the previous preface, *The Greek State.* There Nietzsche seemed to be interested in fostering institutions (in particular, the state) that would generate and prepare geniuses. This interest is an attempt to discern the causes of genius and to arrange circumstances to concentrate and bolster those causes. Nietzsche pursued the causes of human greatness throughout his writing career. Often, in his published works, Nietzsche characterizes great human beings as "atavisms." This is an attempt to give a causal account for their strangeness, rarity, and extraordinary appearance. "I prefer to understand the rare human beings of an age as suddenly appearing late ghosts of past cultures and their powers, as atavisms of a people and its mores – that way one can really *understand* something about them!" (*The Gay Science*, section 10). Nietzsche seeks the causes of human greatness "to prepare great ventures and overall attempts of discipline and cultivation by way of putting an end to that gruesome dominion of nonsense and accident that has so far been called 'history'" (*Beyond Good and Evil*, section 203; cf. *Philosophy in the Tragic Age of the Greeks,* section 1). The idea of a great chain of geniuses is not the idea of the Übermensch, who is singular and historical – one being is sought such as has never yet existed, who will transcend human beings and to whom human beings will be laughingstocks. What is sought in *The Greek State* aims more at eternity, despite all the obstacles in the way of living (and dying) beings participating in anything eternal. This concern persists in Nietzsche in some form up to the very end of his career. "The problem I raise here is not what ought to succeed mankind in the sequence of species . . . but what type of human being one ought to *breed*, ought to *will*, as more valuable. . . . This more valuable type has existed often enough already: but as a lucky accident, as an exception, never as *willed*" (*The Anti-Christ*, section 3). Given the importance to humanity of the genius and the participation in the eternal that it may offer, Nietzsche finds the accidental emergence of geniuses "gruesome," and he seeks to put an end to the accidental by making the state into a genius-making machine. But what exactly is so gruesome about genius if it was the case that it was accidental and, consequently, could neither be understood nor produced?

The case that Nietzsche is considering in *The Relation of Schopenhauerian Philosophy to a German Culture* seems precisely to be that of the accidental appearance of a genius. Is Schopenhauer's appearance gruesome? One objection to the accidental is that it is unpredictable and uncontrollable. Putting an end to the role of accident in the appearance of genius would mean that one could reliably have a genius whenever needed or desired. But how many geniuses do we need? And do we need living, or present, ones? The idea of culture is that the greatness of the *past* is *still* great for me. Nietzsche presents Schopenhauer as "here," but Schopenhauer the man had already been dead for over twelve years. If accident were only objectionable because it is unreliable, that objection would seem moot when the needed accident had in fact delivered the needed genius. But Nietzsche not only objects to the accident of past genius, he also objects to the nonsense. Schopenhauer is "here," but he does not fit in. It is not right to try to make Schopenhauer profess all the opinions of the contemporary non-culture. For Schopenhauer to be great for me does not depend wholly upon Schopenhauer – "the way that greatness has to go toward immortality . . . leads through human brains" (*The Pathos of Truth*, paragraph 3). What Nietzsche calls the "fundamental thought of culture" in *The Pathos of Truth*, he calls "a task, the problem of culture" in a preliminary draft, and he says this problem is "conditioned by the difficulty of its *tradition*" (*Preliminary Draft* #1).

Perhaps this is why Nietzsche was interested in Germany? As the opening of the preface suggests, Germany is not only "lowly" but "dear." Germany may have no culture "now," but it seems to have had a rich tradition in the past. Foreigners who admire Germany know it as a land of "great individuals, works, and actions." Chains are not made up of isolated links. Cultures need forging; they need making and (sometimes) remaking. Things that are difficult to unite need to be put together. To make the greatness of the past "still living, bright, and great" for me it must be organically connected to my present life. But if greatness is eternal it does not share the essential characteristics of the living. "Infinity & inexhaustibility is the essence of greatness – no time will use it up" (*Preliminary Draft* #1). When Nietzsche writes Schopenhauer's name at the end of the preface, he separates the Arthur from the *Schopenhauer* by his emphasis. Culture is making the eternal live and breathe – it is mixing the timebound with the timeless. Arthur is dead. Is Schopenhauer still alive? Can he be made alive through some kind of effort?

The first kind of effort that seems to be recommended is to seek the culture that belongs to Schopenhauer the philosopher, presumably in order to remake Germany into such a culture. But the preface tells us almost nothing about Schopenhauer, either as a man or as a philosopher. We are told only that he is the single German philosopher of the century. But perhaps the who of Schopenhauer is not as important as the what, and perhaps that what is to be construed in the most universal terms. Nietzsche blames Plato's approach in the *Republic*, because "he did not place the genius in his universal concept at the peak, rather only the genius of wisdom." Why then when it is Nietzsche's turn does he point immediately to a philosopher? Perhaps even this, as Nietzsche says of Plato's approach, "may not be thoroughly reckoned among the main features" (*Preliminary Draft* #7) of Nietzsche's approach. Perhaps for the purposes of this preface, and for the purposes of linking the eternal past to the living context of the timebound present, we do not need to understand anything about Schopenhauer other than that he is a genius. We are told nothing here of any details or qualities of Schopenhauer's philosophy. And perhaps we do not need to be told. Could it be that the culture that corresponds to Schopenhauer would correspond to any genius, or could be made to correspond to any genius? What then would be *German* about such a culture?

But is a German culture really what is being sought here? At the very end of the preface, Nietzsche writes something that may point away from state-making or culture-making in any mechanical or material or even social sense. He writes of being able to "foresee" the culture that would correspond to Schopenhauer. This very foreseeing would constitute a judgment of both the seeker himself and of his contemporary, so-called "culture." If we seek the culture that corresponds to Schopenhauer, what then? Will we too be judged? Would this very act of judging situate Schopenhauer for us and thereby make his greatness presently available? Does judgment constitute its own culture, one that transcends time and place? If so, perhaps those with judgment need never find themselves in a place where there is no culture.

MWG

THE RELATION OF SCHOPENHAUERIAN PHILOSOPHY TO A GERMAN CULTURE.

Preface.

In dear lowly Germany culture [Bildung] now lies in the streets so corrupt, envious looks [Scheelsucht] rule so shamelessly in everything great, and the general tumult of those running toward "happiness" sounds so ear numbing, that one must have a strong belief, almost in the sense of credo quia absurdum est,[1] in order here indeed still to hope for a growing culture [Kultur] and before all else to be able to work for the same – publicly teaching in opposition to the "public opinion"[2] of the press. With force must they, those to whom the undying concern with the people lies at heart, free themselves from the impressions that storm in upon them of that which is precisely now present day [Gegenwärtigen] and current [Geltenden] and to excite the appearance as if they reckoned these same things among the indifferent things. They must appear thus, because they want to think, and because a con-

---

1   Latin for "I believe because it is absurd." This is a phrase commonly attributed to the theologian Tertullian (c. 160–220 A.D.). This is likely a misquote (see Timothy Barnes, *Tertullian: A Historical and Literary Study*, Oxford, 1971, p. 223, footnote 4). In *De Carne Christi* (*On the Flesh of Christ*), Tertullian writes: credibile est, quia ineptum est, "It is credible, because it is silly" in response to the claim, et mortuus est dei filius, "The son of God died."

2   More literally, "public opining." Cf. *David Strauss the Confessor and the Writer*, section 1.

trary view and a confused one, probably indeed, disturbs their thinking with the trumpet blast of a sound mixed with the glory of war, but before all else, because they want *to believe* in that which is German and would lose along with this belief their strength [Kraft]. These believing ones are not to be blamed if they very much from the distance and from above look down on the land of their promises! They shy away from the experiences that the well-wishing foreigner exposes if he now lives among Germans and is compelled to wonder how little German life corresponds to those great individuals, works, and actions that he, in his well-wishing, had learned to revere as the authentically German. Whenever the German cannot elevate himself into the great he makes less than a mediocre impression. Even the famous German science, in which a number of the most useful domestic and familial virtues, loyalty, self-limitation, diligence, modesty, purity, appear transposed into freer air and at the same time transfigured, is still in no way the result of these virtues; considered up close [aus der Nähe betrachtet] the motive force [Motiv] driving toward unlimited knowledge looks in Germany like a lack, a defect, resembling much more a gap than a superfluity of strength [Kräften], almost like the result of a needy, formless, unlively life and even like a flight from moral smallness and wickedness, to which the German, without such diversions, is subjugated and which also, despite the science, indeed still quite often within the science, breaks forth. Upon the limitation, in living, knowing, and judging, the Germans understand themselves as the true virtuosos of Philistinism; if one wants to carry them over themselves into the sublime,[3] thus they make themselves heavy like lead, and as such lead weights they hang on their truly great ones in order to draw these down out of the ether and to their needy neediness. Perhaps this Philistine-complacency may only be the degeneration of a true [ächten] German virtue – a heartfelt sinking into the singular, the small, the most near, and into the mysteries of the individual – but this moldy virtue is now worse than the most obvious vice, especially since one has been blithely conscious even now of this quality of hearts to the point of the literary self-glorification. Now the *"cultured"* [Gebildeten] among the well-known so cultivated [kultivirten]

3   Or, "the elevated."

Germans, and the *"Philistines,"* among the well-known so uncultivated Germans, publicly shake hands and strike an agreement with one another, how henceforth one must write, make poems, paint, make music, and even philosophize, indeed rule in order neither to stand too distant from the "culture" [Bildung] of the one nor tread too closely to the "complacency" of the other. This, one now calls "The German Culture [Cultur] of the Present Day"; whereby it would still only be to be ascertained by which marks is that "cultured man" [Gebildete] to be recognized, according to which we know that his milk-brother, the German Philistine, without bashfulness, at the same time according to lost innocence, gives himself now to all the world to be recognized as such.

The educated human being [Gebildete] is now before all else *historically* educated [gebildet]: through his historical consciousness he saves himself in the face of the sublime,[4] which the Philistine succeeds in doing through his "complacency." No more the enthusiasm which history excites – as indeed Goethe may have supposed[5] – rather exactly the blunting [Abstumpfen] of all enthusiasm is now the goal of these admirers [Bewunderer] of the nil admirari,[6] when they seek to grasp [begreifen] everything historically; but one must call to them: "You are

4   Or, "the elevated"
5   "The best thing that we have from history is the enthusiasm that it excites." Goethe, *Aus Wilhelm Meisters Wanderjahren*, Bk 2, in "Considerations according to the Sense of Wanderers"; reused in Goethe *Maxims and Reflections*, 495. Cf. *David Strauss the Confessor and the Writer*, section 2.
6   Latin for "admire nothing"; this is from the beginning of Horace's *Epistles*, number VI, to Numicius: Nil admirari prope res est una, Numici, solaque quae facere et servare beatum. "'Admire nothing' – that is perhaps the one and only thing, Numicius, that can make a man happy and keep him so." This is a Latin version of the Greek τὸ μηδὲν θαυμάζειν, "wonder at nothing," of Protagoras or the ἡ ἀθαυμαστία, "non-wondering," of some other philosophers (see Strabo, *The Geography*, i.3.21); it is close to the ἀθαμβία, "non-astonishment," or ἐυθυμία, "cheerfulness," of Democritus (see Cicero *De finibus* V. 29.87) and the ἀταραξία, "calmness," of the Epicureans and the ἀπάθεια, "apathy," of the Stoics. Cf. *David Strauss the Confessor and the Writer*, section 2; *Richard Wagner in Bayreuth*, section 6.

the fools of all centuries! History will only make confessions to you that are worthy of you! The world has been at all times full of trivialities and nothingnesses: your historical lusts [Gelüste] reveal themselves as just these and precisely only these. You can by the thousands pounce upon an epoch – you will hunger afterwards as before and you will be able to praise to yourself your kind of starved [angehungerter] health. Illam ipsam quam iactant sanitatem non firmitate sed ieinnie consequuntur. Dial. de orator.c.25.[7] Everything essential, history has not wanted to say to you; rather mocking and invisible it stood next to you, pressing into the hand of this one a state action, to that one a diplomatic report, to another a period [Jahreszahl][8] or an etymology or a pragmatic spider-web. Do you really believe history can be reckoned up together like an addition problem, and do you hold your common understanding and your mathematical education as good enough for that? How must it annoy you to hear, that others explain things, out of the most familiar times, that you will never and by no means grasp!"

If now to this self-naming historical culture devoid of enthusiasm [Begeisterung] and to a philistinism hostile to and full of venom toward everything great yet that third, brutal, and excited cooperative [Genossenschaft] comes – those who run toward "happiness" – thus there will be in summa such a confounded outcry and such a limb-contorting turmoil that the thinker will flee into the loneliest wilderness with stopped-up ears and bound eyes – therein he may see what those never will see, where he must hear what resounds to him out of all the depths of nature and down from the stars. Here he confers with the great problems hovering near to him, whose voices ring out to be sure, just as much cheerless-fearful [ungemütlich-furchtbar] as unhistorical-eternal. The weak flee backwards before their cold breath, and the calculating run right through them without noticing them. But it comes out worst with them for the "cultured" [Gebildeten], who occasionally

7   Latin for "even their health which they parade they obtain not through strength but through fasting"; Cornelius Tacitus, *Dialogue on Oratory*, Ch. 23 (not 25 as Nietzsche's text indicates). Tacitus's line reads a little differently from Nietzsche's: illam ipsam quam iactant sanitatem non firmitate, sed ieiunio consequuntur. Nietzsche quotes this line again in *David Strauss the Confessor and the Writer*, section 11.
8   More literally, "count of years."

gives himself in his way serious trouble about them. For him these ghosts [Gespenster] metamorphose into concept webs [Begriffsgespinnste] and hollow, sound figures. Grasping after them, he fancies to have philosophy, in order to seek after them, he clambers around in the so-called history of philosophy – and if he finally has collected together and accumulated a whole cloudbank of such abstractions and templates – thus it may befall him that a true thinker blocks his way and – blows it away. Desperate inconvenience, to meddle with philosophy as a "cultured" man! From time to time indeed it appears to him as if the impossible combination of philosophy with that which now boasts of itself as "German Culture" [Kultur] has become possible; any hermaphroditic creature flirts and ogles around between both spheres and confounds the fantasy on this side and on that. But in the meantime the Germans are, if they do not want to let themselves be confounded, to be given *one* recommendation. They may all together ask what they now name "culture" [Bildung]: is *this* the hoped-for German culture [Kultur], so serious and creative, so redeeming for the German spirit, so purifying for German virtues, that their single philosopher in this century, Arthur *Schopenhauer*, should have to profess [bekennen] it?

Here you have the philosopher – now seek the culture [Kultur] belonging to him! And if you are able to foresee what kind of culture [Kultur] that must be, which would correspond to such a philosopher, now thus you have, in this foreseeing, already, over all your culture [Bildung] and over you yourselves – *passed judgment*!

CONTEST AS CONTEXT

What is humanity? What do we want it to be? Nietzsche suggests that when we speak of humanity, we tacitly reveal a desire to be something other than what we are. More explicitly, we reveal a desire to be distinguished from nature, which we regard as fearsome and agonistic. Perhaps we wish to think of human beings as separate from nature, because, if they are, then the possibility may be available to human beings to create a world of perpetual peace, a world where all that is savage in us may be left behind.

When Nietzsche asks himself what humanity is, he comes face to face with a different possibility. The human being, he concludes, cannot be separated from nature. What the human being is and what nature is have grown "inseparably together," so that the "human being, in his highest and noblest forces, is wholly nature and carries her double character in himself." The highest human being, therefore, has characteristics we would deem genuinely human in addition to the ferocity and savagery we might wish to associate with nature alone. But then Nietzsche adds an intriguing suggestion. Perhaps the difficulty is not simply that one cannot have what is considered human without having what is ferocious. Perhaps the difficulty is also that ferociousness and what is deemed inhuman or sub-human are actually the "fruitful soul out of which alone all humanity can grow forth." The possibility that this might be true obligates us to reconsider the condemnation of the destructive drives.

Nietzsche finds the ancient Greeks to be an appropriate means of investigating this question. This is likely because he thinks their culture is the greatest that we have ever known, and it produced the highest and noblest human beings that have existed. Nietzsche calls the ancient Greeks the "most human human beings." This suggests that he thinks they have those qualities held to be genuinely human to a degree that has not been surpassed. In spite of, or perhaps because of, this superlative humanity, they also have "a strain of cruelty, of tigerish lust to annihilate, in them." Thus, the most *human* human beings have not left behind those qualities that those who speak of humanity would like to eradicate from the human soul. What is particularly significant for Nietzsche's inquiry, however, is that the Greeks do not seem to be ashamed of their ferocity, and they do not seem to wish to eradicate it.

The Greeks' ferocity is apparent in their "whole history just as much so in their mythology" and their art more generally. Homer describes battle scenes in careful detail so that the Greeks can re-live these wars repeatedly. The Greek sculptor stamps "ever again war and battles in countless repetitions, stretched-out human bodies, whose sinews are strained by hatred or by the wantonness of triumph, crooked wounded, rattling out [their] dying." The historian Thucydides describes how callous and brutal the Greeks can be when they are victorious in war. They can slaughter an entire city of defeated men and sell the women and children into slavery, and they seem able to regard these actions with a clear conscience as things done "according to the *right* of war."

We must ask, along with Nietzsche, why the Greeks "exult" in such images. Why do they seem *to want* to relive them? Nietzsche seems to suggest that a partial answer lies in the fact that Greeks feel the need to give freer rein to their ferocious drives in order to maintain their health. It is as if restraining the ferocious drives during peaceful times causes these drives to build up in the human being until eventually they make the Greek feel "compressed and swollen." When this happens, the Greek must find an opportunity to release these drives so that the swelling that has resulted from their containment does not become unhealthy for him or for his society. The tiger that is part of the human being is allowed to hurry forth with "a voluptuous cruelty" in his "fearsome eye."

However, Nietzsche is not satisfied with the argument that the Greeks act ferociously simply because they must. They seem to regard ferocity and strife not as necessary evils, but as things that are good.

This suspicion compels Nietzsche to conclude that we do not yet understand the Greek exultation of war "Greekly enough."

According to Nietzsche, Homer will not take us to the depths that are required for the kind of insight we want. Homer's poetry is already too artistic to allow us to see clearly what must be seen. His works already lift us "off and way over the pure material melding by the extraordinary artistic determinateness, rest, and purity of lines" so that the world appears "lighter, milder, warmer, its human beings . . . better and more sympathetic." In other words, Homer is too expert a liar. Given this, Nietzsche turns to Hesiod, whose *Theogony* tells of the generation of the gods and ultimately of the human world. Can such a poem teach us something about the Greek understanding of the original state of things?

In Hesiod, Nietzsche finds a "fancy accustomed to the horrible." Hesiod describes the original, primary condition as one ruled solely by the "*children of the night*, quarrel, lust, deception, old age, and death." Nietzsche asks us to condense and darken this world in order to recede even further into what the unedited Greek view of the world might have been before the "softening" that flowed over Hellas from Delphi. The picture is dark indeed: a cosmos of apparently endless destruction, strife, and disorder. Nietzsche suggests that this conception of reality would "*squeeze* a mythic world out of us" in which "Uranus, Kronos, and Zeus and the battles between the Titans must be thought of as a relief; battle is, in this brooding atmosphere, grace, salvation; the cruelty of victory is the peak of life's jubilation." This is Nietzsche's suggestion as to why the Greeks revere the images of destruction and war. Against the backdrop of a chaotic world, war is regarded as "grace" and "salvation." However, the reason why war comes as relief against such a backdrop remains largely or entirely opaque.

Before offering a more explicit answer, Nietzsche moves on. He notes that nothing so separates one world from another as the coloration of the "individual ethical concepts," such as Eris (Strife) and envy, that flow from that world's view of battle and victory. With this, the question is at least clarified, even if Nietzsche's answer to it is not: if we are to understand why the Greeks do not condemn the ferocious drives that those who speak of humanity would like to exclude, then we must gain a greater understanding of how they conceived of war.

In *Works and Days*, Hesiod indicates that the Greeks think there are two forms of Eris, each of which has a wholly different temperament from the other. One Eris "promotes bad war and discord, the cruel one." Though this bad Eris comes unwelcome to human beings, she is honored by them "under the yoke of need . . . according to the decree of the immortals." Though Nietzsche speaks as if he is simply translating Hesiod, he appears to make some changes to the poem that may be significant. Using Hesiod's voice, he characterizes this Eris as the elder, but in the editions available to us Hesiod actually names the good Eris as the older of the two. If Nietzsche makes this change, does he do so because he thinks it is more representative of the Greek view of the cosmos to say that its primary condition is one of bad strife? Whether it legitimately reflects the Greek view, or whether Nietzsche changes it for other reasons, the change has the effect of making the first condition of the cosmos imperfect and, at least for human beings, bad. To put it bluntly, the cosmos needs fixing.

Hesiod presents the good Eris as one that was "planted" by the "son of Kronos . . . in the roots of the earth and among men." Again, Nietzsche makes some changes to the poem. This time, he names Zeus directly as the one who planted this Eris among men. He omits the circumlocution that reminds us that Zeus is the son of Kronos or Time [Chronos]. Could it be that by changing this reference to Zeus Nietzsche wants to emphasize Zeus's independence from his father? Is this rebellion against time comparable to a human rebellion against time?

In the *Theogony*, Hesiod tells us that Kronos sought to retain his kingship by swallowing his children, whom he believed might overthrow him. His treatment of his offspring is comparable to that of his father, Uranus. Uranus buried his fearsome, hundred-armed children in Earth. Zeus also seeks to retain his rule, but he finds another way to confront the threat of being overthrown. Following the advice of Earth and Night, Zeus swallows his wife, Metis (resource, cunning).

The strife that Zeus exhibits is to be distinguished from the violent behavior of Uranus and Kronos. All three gods act so as to place limits on the primordial state of chaos or bad strife; however, the violence exhibited by Uranus and Kronos when they try to secure their rule against their children seems only to be an effort to maintain the status quo by containing these children. Zeus confronts the threat to his rule by trying to become better than his offspring. Swallowing Metis is surely a violent act, but by it Zeus seems intent not on destroying his offspring or his wife but on incorporating his wife into himself. Metis is wisest among both gods and men. By swallowing her, Zeus literally combines his might with her wisdom. Metis can and does now advise Zeus from within. Thus, by swallowing Metis, one might say that he has found a way to use strife so as to promote his improvement, which is a form of growth.

Zeus may have planted good strife among humans so that we could imitate his life-promoting action. Hesiod says the good Eris is good for human beings because she motivates them to strive to become better: "Even the potter resents the potter and the carpenter the carpenter, the beggar envies the beggar and the singer the singer." Like war, envy and resentment are forms of strife; yet, Hesiod depicts them as good. Nietzsche notes that scholars of our day do not understand why Hesiod speaks approvingly of the potter's envy and resentment of another potter. Rather than entertaining the idea that the Greeks might have had a different conception of strife, these scholars conclude that the verses must be inauthentic.

Nietzsche objects to such a conclusion on the grounds that the same approval of envy can be found in other works from antiquity, including the works of Aristotle. In Aristotle's *Rhetoric*, which is most likely the work to which Nietzsche alludes, Aristotle does not speak of two forms of Eris. He actually uses two distinct terms, which are jealousy or emulation (ὁ ζῆλος) on the one hand and envy (τὸ φθονεῖν) on the other, to discuss what Hesiod refers to as the two forms of Eris. Apparently, Aristotle introduces these terms in order to elaborate upon what Hesiod says, and the way in which Aristotle defines them seems to correspond to what Hesiod calls good and bad envy. Because Nietzsche may be correct in his assessment of the confusion surrounding jealousy and envy, it may be useful to examine Aristotle's more detailed account of these two passions and their differences.

Aristotle implies that jealousy belongs to beings that are incomplete with respect to the good, and who strive to obtain the good they lack. Because jealousy involves both a love of the good and the effort to acquire it for oneself, jealousy is a good passion experienced by good human beings:

> Jealousy is pain caused by seeing the presence, in persons whose nature is like our own, of good things that are highly valued. . . . [B]ut it is felt not because others have these goods, but because we have not got them ourselves. It is therefore a good feeling felt by good persons. . . . Jealousy makes us take steps to secure the good things in question. (Aristotle, *Rhetoric* [1388a29–1385b5])

Jealousy is wholly without malice toward the possessor of the good thing. If one is jealous of a wise man for his wisdom, for example, this does not mean that one hates the wise man for having wisdom; rather, one is motivated to try to become wise oneself. The jealous human being might regard the possessor of the good thing as a rival if the good in question is limited; and competition for a limited good might arouse such passions as anger, aggression, or even envy, but these passions are not an inherent part of jealousy. In fact, one can reasonably infer that jealousy is likely to inspire admiration in the jealous human being for the one who possesses the good thing. It may even evoke in the jealous human being feelings of friendship or goodwill toward the possessor. This is because jealousy depends upon the jealous person's assumption that he is similar to the possessor of the good thing. His belief in this similarity is what makes him think that he too can acquire the good that the other has. To the extent that the jealous human being loves the good, thinks of himself as a good person, and identifies with the one who has the good thing, he will think the one for whom he feels jealousy is also a good man, and he will love him for his goodness.

Unlike jealousy, envy is a form of malice and, to the extent that one suffers from it, one is quite simply bad. Envy actually makes the one who suffers from it take steps to prevent others from having good things. It does not stimulate the envious person to acquire the good; rather, the envious person merely wishes to harm the one whom he envies. There is therefore nothing constructive or elevating about envy: "Envy is pain at the sight of such good fortune as consists in the good things. . . . [W]e feel it . . . not with the idea of getting something for ourselves, but because the other people have it" (*Rhetoric* 1387b20–25).

Having made this distinction between jealousy (good envy) and envy (bad envy), we are better able to see what the difference is between good and bad strife more generally. Good strife seems to share the qualities that make jealousy good. It ultimately aims at producing something better or higher. By contrast, bad strife is simply destructive. It aims to annihilate that which is better or higher. Thus, when Nietzsche suggests that the Greeks found relief in Uranus, Kronos, and Zeus and in the battles of the Titans in the face of a world ruled by the *"children of darkness,"* he may mean that the Greeks thought rule by the children of darkness was characterized only by bad strife. The battles of Uranus, Kronos, Zeus and the Titans may have been regarded by the Greeks as efforts to give a more articulate form to this simply destructive strife. This articulation seems to come as a relief to human beings; it seems to be life-promoting whereas the more fundamental state of chaos or bad strife was not.

The goodness of the good strife should not make us lose sight of the fact that it is violent. In order to create something new, the old order must be destroyed. Parts must be re-arranged, new parts may have to be made by pulling apart existing wholes, and parts that were separate may have to be forced into new wholes. All of these acts are violent, and, as such, they require the ferocious drives that we might wish to exclude from what is considered genuinely human.

And when faced with such violence, might one not still object that war and all other forms of destruction never truly result in anything good? Nietzsche tells us that when faced with a "world of battle and cruelty," those from India and the Orient became disgusted with existence. Other, perhaps more modern, readers may wonder whether in the face of such a world it might not be more reasonable to conclude that perpetual peace rather than so-called good war is the true grace and salvation for human beings. War always gives birth to more of the same, and so it can never be good.

If we compare the idea that salvation would lie in perpetual peace with the idea that an existence of ceaseless turmoil is disgusting, we find that they actually share a similar presupposition that does not seem to be shared by the ancient Greeks Nietzsche describes. The idea that there may be perpetual peace and the belief that the world is in a state of constant war both rest on a belief that a condition may be infinite, eternal, or unmeasured. Furthermore, both positions assume implicitly that human beings can or do live in one of these unmeasured states. Do the ancient Greeks, as Nietzsche presents or even reveals them, hold such ideas? Perhaps the closest the Greeks come to such unmeasured and perhaps immeasurable states is in their thoughts about the divine. However, the Greeks do not seem to think even these divine beings live in an unlimited condition of either peace or strife. Battles come; they are resolved; and strife arises again.

If we move from the realm of divine beings to that of human beings, it seems we have reduced or removed entirely that which is unlimited, for we are no longer dealing with eternal beings. Rather, human life is limited, just like the periods of war and peace that occur among human beings. This suggests that the Greeks may have thought the world, or at least the natural and human world that is intelligible to us, is a measured world, a world of limits.

In measurement, we may have the key to understanding what Nietzsche means when he says the Greeks' view of the primary state of things would "squeeze a mythic world out of us in which Uranus, Kronos, and Zeus and the battles of the Titans must be thought of as a relief." These gods, their battles, and their victories impose measure or limits upon the primordial condition of chaos or near chaos. The imposition of measure that results from victorious war may be welcomed by us as "the peak of life's jubilation" because we are measuring beings. We find our home in measurement and in a measured world. We must separate one thing from another and compare it to other things so that it can assume a place in the order of things as it presents itself to us. This is how the world is made intelligible to us.

What it means to have a measured world and what it means to suggest human beings find their home in such a world may become more apparent if we consider *Genesis*, which is perhaps a more familiar account of the divine origin of the world. God's creative activity consists largely or wholly in division and separation, and it is by separation and division that measurement comes to be. What is wholly unarticulated and without boundaries is infinite or unlimited. As soon as one thing is divided or separated from some other thing, measure is introduced. This is what we see God doing in the act of creation. He separates light from darkness to make the first day; he separates the waters to make dry land; by division, he makes Heaven and Earth; and he separates a rib from Adam in order to make a companion for him that is similar in kind (*Genesis* 1–2). God's creative acts suggest that he too may be a measuring being, but the decisive evidence that he is so comes in his valuation of his own work: "God saw that it was good" (*Genesis* 2: 19–20). The concept that something is good requires one to compare the thing in question with something else and to rate it in relation to this other thing. This measure of what is good or bad is arguably the most significant aspect of what it means to say a human being is a measuring being.

That measure, and measure of the good in particular, is the crux of what Nietzsche has in mind when he speaks of the Greeks' jubilation in battle and victory is further suggested by the fact that immediately after discussing the Greeks' jubilation in victory Nietzsche explicitly introduces the subject of justice, which is a form of measure that is also clearly moral. According to Nietzsche, this specific kind of measure arose out of victory. Ultimately, battle lays the foundation for a nobler culture: "[I]n truth the concept of Greek justice has developed itself out of murder and atonement for murder, thus also a nobler culture takes its first victory laurel from the altar of atonement for murder."

Does measuring, and therefore the human being as a measuring being, depend upon strife? Every time one compares one thing to another, one is, in a way, setting up a relationship of opposition. However, this does not make the Greeks disgusted with life, nor does it make them yearn for perpetual peace. Perhaps it is because they understand the human being as a measuring being that they regard strife, or at least good strife, as an *affirmation* of life. Perhaps this is the reason Nietzsche thinks they can say where others cannot that a "life of battle and victory" lacks nothing. Even further, a life without strife may very literally be no life at all.

Competition may augment the Greeks' vitality by providing them with a context in which measurements can be taken. One human being competes with another, and the winner of the contest emerges as the standard by which excellence is measured and thereby made intelligible. This standard does not have to exist in a living human being, nor does the Greek have to compete solely with the living. He can and does also look to the dead for worthy contestants and for his standard of excellence. The contest, which is to say good strife, directs the life of the Greek individual and Greek culture. More specifically, it has a vitalizing effect on the Greek soul and Greek culture because it balances creative and destructive activity.

Nietzsche implies that the creative effects of the strife that belongs to contest are particularly apparent when contest is lacking. This can occur when a Greek human being finds himself so far beyond others that he lacks competitors. Without competitors, he seems to lack a means of measuring his activity and thereby directing it. One might say that in the absence of the contest he lacks a context in which his actions are made intelligible to himself. In this condition, he will degenerate into that primary state of chaos described by Hesiod: "[T]ake away . . . the contest form from Greek life, thus we see immediately in that pre-Homeric abyss a horrible wilderness of hatred and lust to annihilate. . . . [The Greek] was not able to bear fame and fortune without further contest." The absence of good strife, whether in peacetime or in war, has an enervating effect on human life.

The health of Greek culture is promoted and sustained in a manner that is similar to that of the individual. Thus, Nietzsche seems to liken culture to a living thing. The culture – its being – is sustained by the activity that is the contest. Because the Greeks feel "the necessity of the contest if the health of the state should endure," they take steps to ensure that the contest continues. Ostracism is such a step. A human being who so far exceeds his fellows that he has no competitors must be ostracized because he exhausts the contest, and thereby endangers the "eternal basis of life of the Hellenic state." We may re-state this conclusion in the language of measure: the human being who has no competitors cannot be measured because he lacks a context. He therefore threatens the very concept of measure, which in turn threatens the continuation of life-promoting, as opposed to anti-life, strife in the Greek culture and in the Greek individual. The one assumption upon which the Greek contest depends is that "in a natural order of things, there are always *more* geniuses who reciprocally incite [each other] to deeds, as they also reciprocally hold [each other] within the borders of nature."

Beyond the borders of nature dwell the gods. Though they seem to be measuring beings, they are unmeasured by us. Perhaps it is for this reason that they are regarded by the Greeks as inappropriate competitors for human beings. We are transient, our very existence is measured, but the gods are divine and may ultimately be immeasurable. If this is so, then they seem to stand at the outer limit of the natural, measured world. They separate what is measured from what is unmeasured. Nietzsche maintains that this separation does not alienate the Greek from his gods. Rather, it is this comparison that creates a relationship between the Greek and his gods: "[the gods'] significance is therewith circumscribed in opposition, that with them the human being may *never* dare a contest, he whose soul blushes jealously against every other living being." The gods define the realm in which the human being properly lives and acts. Nietzsche seems to argue that the Greek's knowledge of his place in a measured world actually gives him the freedom to act. The modern human being no longer circumscribes himself in a measured world, or at least he does not do so to the same degree as the ancient Greek. He gazes up toward the infinite. But infinity is unmeasured, and so it cannot give him a goal. Thus, while the modern human being may come closer to having freedom *from* measure, he is also typically less free to act: "The modern human being . . . is generally crossed by infinity like the swift-footed Achilles in the parable of the Eleatic Zeno: infinity hems him in, he does not once catch up with the turtle."

The effort to isolate what we may wish to consider genuinely human from strife is an effort to enter the realm of the unlimited. The ancient Greeks might call this hubristic. Nietzsche calls it impossible, and suggests it is foolish.

LvB

HOMER'S CONTEST

Preface.

If one speaks of *humanity*, thus at bottom lies the idea that wants to be that which *separates* and distinguishes the human being from nature. But in reality there is no such separation: the things named "natural" qualities and those named genuinely "human" have inseparably grown together. The human being, in his highest and noblest forces [Kräften], is wholly nature and carries her uncanny double character in himself. His fearsome capacities, held as they are as inhuman, are perhaps even the fruitful soil out of which alone all humanity can grow forth into emotions, deeds, and works.

Thus the Greeks, the most human [humansten] human beings of ancient times, have a strain [Zug] of cruelty, of tigerish lust to annihilate, in them: a strain which even is very visible to us in that mirror image of the Hellenes overgrown into a grotesque, in Alexander the Great, but also in their whole history just as much so in their mythology, which must put into anxiety us who come up against it with the soft concept of modern humanity. When Alexander had the feet of the brave defender of Gaza, Batis, bored through, his body bound, living, to his chariot, in order to drag him around under the scorn of his soldiers:[1] thus is this the disgust-arousing caricature of Achilles, who mistreated the corpse of Hector nightly through a similar dragging around; but even this strain [Zug] has for us something offensive and horrible

---

1   According to Hegesius of Magnesias as cited in F. Jacoby, *Die Fragmente der griechischen Historiker* (Leiden, 1940–1941), 142.5.

[Grausen] infused into it. We look here into the abyss of hatred. With the same feeling we stand, so to speak, also before the bloody and insatiable self-laceration of two Greek parties, e.g., in the Corcyrean revolution.[2] When the victor in a battle of cities, according to the *right* of war, executes the collected male citizenry and sells all the women and children into slavery, thus we see, in the sanction of such a right, that the Greek thought [erachtet] of letting his hatred stream outward completely as a serious necessity; in such moments he alleviated the feeling that had become compressed and swollen: the tiger hurried forth, a voluptuous cruelty looked out of his fearsome eye. Why must the Greek sculptor stamp ever again war and battles in countless repetitions, stretched-out human bodies, whose sinews are strained by hatred or by the wantonness[3] of triumph, crooked wounded, rattling out [their] dying? Why did the whole Greek world exult at the images of battle of the *Iliad*? I fear that we do not understand this "Greekly" enough, indeed that we would shudder if we should for once understand it Greekly.

But what lies *behind* the Homeric world as the birth womb of everything Hellenic? In *this* we will already have been lifted off and away over the pure material melding by the extraordinarily artistic determinateness, rest, and purity of the lines: its colors appear to us, through an artistic deception, lighter, milder, warmer, its human beings, in this colorful, warm lighting, better and more sympathetic – but where do we look when we, no longer led and protected by the hand of Homer, stride backward into the pre-Homeric world? Only into night and horror [Grauen], into the product of a fancy accustomed to the horrible. Which earthly existence do these loathsome-fearful Theogonistic myths [Sagen] mirror again: a life, over which alone the *children of the night*, quarrel, lust, deception, old age, and death rule. Let us think of the hard-to-breathe air of the Hesiodic poem still condensed and darkened and without all the softening and purifying that streamed out over Hellas from Delphi and from numerous seats of the gods: let us mix this thickened, Boeothian air with the dark volup-

2   Thucydides, Book III, paragraphs 70-85; cf. also *The Wanderer and His Shadow*, section 31.
3   Or "arrogance" or "high spirits."

tuousness of the Etruscan; then such a reality would *squeeze* a mythic world out of us in which Uranus, Kronos, and Zeus and the battles of the Titans must be thought of as a relief [Erleichterung]; battle is, in this brooding atmosphere, grace [Heil], salvation [Rettung]; the cruelty of victory is the peak of life's jubilation. And as in truth the concept of Greek justice [Rechte] has developed itself out of *murder* and atonement for murder, thus also a nobler culture takes its first victory laurel from the altar of atonement for murder. Afterwards that bloody age cut a deep tidal furrow into Hellenic history. The names of Orpheus,[4] of Musäus[5] and their cults betray the results to which the uninterrupted spectacle [Anblick] of a world of battle and cruelty pressed – to disgust in existence, to interpretation of this existence as an expiating punishment, to belief in the identity of being there [Dasein][6] and being guilty [Verschuldetsein]. But precisely these results are not specifically Hellenic: in them Greece touches upon India and generally upon the Orient. The Hellenic genius had ready still another answer to the question, "What wants a life of battle and victory?" And it gives this answer in the whole breadth of Greek history.

In order to understand it, we must set out from the fact that the Greek genius considered the at-one-time so fearsomely present drive as allowed and as *entitled*: the thought that a life with such a drive as its root would not be worth living was located during the Orphic turn. Battle and the pleasure in victory became recognized: and nothing divides the Greek world from ours so much as the *coloration*, leading from here, of individual ethical concepts, e.g., of *Eris*[7] and of *envy*.

4   Orpheus was the mythical son of Apollo and a Muse. He was a singer of wondrous power. He used this power to descend into Hades to rescue his lover Eurydice but failed. As a mortal who had traveled to the underworld, he became known as a possessor of secret or special wisdom. He was killed by Bacchic maenads, and the Bacchic mystery cults adopted him as their figurehead.

5   Musäus, whose name means "he of the Muses" was also a mythical singer, closely connected to Orpheus and regarded by some as his son. Poems attributed to Musäus are associated with the Eleusian mystery cults.

6   Or "existence."

7   This is the name of the personified concept of strife or discord.

As the traveling Pausanias on his wanderings through Greece visited the Helicon, an original ancient exemplar of the first didactic poem of the Greeks, the "Works and Days" of Hesiod, was shown to him, inscribed upon lead plates and badly ravaged by time and weather.[8] Yet he recognized this much, that it, in opposition to the usual exemplars, did *not* possess at its peak that little hymn to Zeus;[9] rather it began immediately with the declaration, "There are two goddesses Eris upon the earth."[10] This is one of the Hellenic thoughts most worthy of noting and is worthy to be impressed upon those coming in right at the entrance gate of Hellenic ethics. "If one has understanding, one wants to praise the one Eris just as much as to blame the other; for these two goddesses have a wholly separate kind of temperament [Gemüthsart]. For the one promotes the bad war and discord, the cruel one! No mortal suffers her willingly; rather under the yoke of need they render the heavy, burdensome Eris honor, according to the decree of the immortals. This one was born, as the older, to black night; but the other one Zeus, ruling on high, planted in the roots of the earth and among men as a much better thing. She drives even the unskilled [ungeschickten] man to work; and when one who lacks property looks

8   Pausanias, *Description of Greece*, Book IX, Ch. 31.4: "The Boeotians dwelling around Helicon hold the tradition that Hesiod wrote nothing but the *Works*, and even of this they reject the prelude to the Muses, saying that the poem begins with the account of the Erises." W. H. S. Jones, translator. Cambridge: Harvard University Press, 1961.

9   The part lacking is the first ten lines of the *Works and Days*: "Muses of Pieria who give glory through song, come thither, tell of Zeus your father and chant his praise. Through him mortal men are famed or unfamed, sung or unsung alike, as great Zeus wills. For easily he makes strong, and easily he brings the strong man low; easily he humbles the proud and raises the obscure, and easily he straightens the crooked and blasts the proud – Zeus who thunders aloft and has his dwelling most high. Attend then with eye and ear, and make judgments straight with righteousness. And I, Perses, would tell of true things." Hugh G. Evelyn-White, translator. Cambridge: Harvard University Press, 1974.

10   *Works and Days*, line 11: Οὐκ ἄρα μοῦνον ἔην Ἐρίδων γένος, ἀλλ' ἐπὶ γαῖαν εἰσὶ δυώ. "So, after all, there is not one species of Eris, but over the earth there are two." Cf. *The Wanderer and His Shadow*, section 29.

upon another who is rich, thus he hurries to sow in a similar way and to plant and to appoint the house well; neighbor competes with neighbor, he strives toward prosperity. This Eris is good for human beings. Even the potter resents the potter and the carpenter the carpenter, the beggar envies the beggar and the singer the singer."[11]

The last two verses, which treat of *odium figulinum*,[12] appear to our scholars as inconceivable in this place [Stelle]. According to their judgment the predicates "resentment" and "envy" fit only to the essence of the bad Eris; wherefore they make no bones [keinen Anstand nehmen] about designating the verses as inauthentic and as winding up in this place [Ort] by accident. But for this they must have been inspired, unnoticed, by another ethic than the Hellenic: for Aristotle feels no offence in the relation of these verses to the good Eris.[13] And not Aristotle alone; rather the collected Greek antiquity

11 This is Nietzsche's translation of *Works and Days*, lines 12–26. Nietzsche seems to make a few changes to the text, at least his translation does not correspond to the texts of Hesiod presently known. Nietzsche changes "love" in line 14 to "suffer" (cf. *Preliminary Drafts* #15 and #16, where Nietzsche has "love"). he changes the birth order to make the bad Eris older – which seems to suit Nietzsche's purposes. He substitutes the proper name "Zeus" for the designation "Son of Kronos" or "Son of Time [Chronos]." Nietzsche omits from line 18 the fact that Zeus lives in the ether (see *Preliminary Draft* #16). He may have changed a bit the sense of how or where Zeus planted the good Eris. He substitutes "human beings" for "mortals" in line 24 (see *Preliminary Drafts* #15 and #16). Finally, Nietzsche has "carpenter" for τέκτονι (artisan or craftsman) in line 25.

12 Latin for "potter's hatred." The Greek here is κεραμεὺς κεραμεῖ κοτέει; Aristotle quotes this at *Rhetoric* 1381b21 and 1388a6, and he alludes to it at *Nicomachean Ethics* 1155a35–b1.

13 In the *Rhetoric* , just after quoting Hesiod at 1388a6, Aristotle soon draws a distinction between envy [τὸ φθονεῖν] and jealousy or emulation [ὁ ζῆλος]: "Emulation therefore is virtuous and characteristic of virtuous men, whereas envy is base and characteristic of base men; for the one, owing to emulation, fits himself to obtain such goods, while the object of the other, owing to envy, is to prevent his neighbor possessing them" (1388a23–26). A little earlier, he put it this way: "And those whose rivals we are, or by whom we wish to be emulated [ζηλοῦσθαι] but not envied [φθονεῖσθαι] – these we either like or wish to be friends with them"

thinks otherwise about resentment and envy than we do and judges like Hesiod, who at one time designates one Eris as evil, namely that one which leads human beings to hostile wars of annihilation against one another, and then again prizes another Eris as good, who as jealousy, resentment, envy entices human beings to action, but not to the action of a war of annihilation, rather to the action of the *contest*. The Greek is *envious* and feels this quality not as a blemish, rather as the effect of a *beneficent* divinity: what a cleft of ethical judgment between us and him! Because he is envious, he also feels with every excess of honor, riches, brilliance, and fortune [Glück], the envious eye of a god rests upon him and he fears this envy; in this case it warns him of the transitoriness of every human lot, he dreads[14] his fortune and offering the best therefrom he humbles himself before the divine envy. This idea [Vorstellung] does not, as it were, alienate him from his gods: their significance is therewith circumscribed in opposition, that with them the human being may *never* dare a contest, he whose soul blushes jealously against every other living being. In the battle of Thamyris with the Muses,[15] of Marsyas with Apollo,[16] in the gripping fate of Niobe[17] appear the terrible opposition to one another of two powers that may never fight with one another, of human being and god.

(1381b24–25), John Hendry Freese, translator. Cambridge: Harvard University Press, 1959.

14 Or "grants."

15 Thamyris was a Thracian singer who boasted he could win a contest even with the Muses. As punishment he was blinded and made to forget his skill. Cf. *Iliad*, Book II, lines 594–595.

16 Marsyas was a satyr or a silenus who either invented the aulos (a flute-like instrument) or snatched it up when Athena discarded it. He challenged Apollo to a competition – his aulos against Apollo's cithara (a kind of lyre). Upon losing, Marsyas was strung from a tree and flayed alive.

17 Niobe was the mythical daughter of Tantalus and wife of Amphion. She had a very large family varying in accounts from five to ten children of each sex. She boasted she was superior to Leto, mother of Apollo and of Artemis, who had only one of each. Apollo shot down all of Niobe's sons and Artemis all of her daughters. The weeping Niobe was turned into a rock on the face of Mount Sipylus with water flowing down it like tears.

But the greater and more sublime[18] a Greek human being is, so much brighter does the ambitious flame break out from him, consuming each one who runs with him on the same course. Aristotle once made a list of such hostile contests in the grand style: among them the most conspicuous example is, that even one dead can still entice a living one to consuming jealousy.[19] Thus namely Aristotle designates the relationship of the Kolophonian Xenophanes[20] to Homer. We do not understand in its strength this assault upon the national hero of the poetic art, if we do not think to ourselves, as later even with Plato, as the root of the assault the monstrous lust even to walk in the place of the overturned poet and to inherit his fame. Every great Hellene passes on the torch of the contest; in each great virtue a new greatness catches fire. If the young Themistocles,[21] in thinking of the laurels of Miltiades[22] could not sleep,[23] thus his early-awakened drive first

18 Or "elevated."

19 In Diogenes Laertes *Lives* II.5.46 (*Life of Socrates*), Diogenes attributes the following to Aristotle, "as Homer was assailed in his lifetime by Syasras, and after his death by Xenophanes of Colophon, so too Hesiod was criticized in his lifetime by Cercops, and after his death by the aforesaid Xenophanes." Harvard University Press, Cambridge 1954, R. D. Hicks translator.

20 Xenophanes of Colophon was a poet, theologian, and natural philosopher who lived around 545 B.C. He attacked Homer and Hesiod for portraying the gods as behaving in ways unbecoming for even mortals.

21 Themistocles (c. 524–459 B.C.) was an Athenian politician and the victorious commander of the Greek forces during the Persian invasion and architect of the battle plan at Salamis, the decisive naval battle.

22 Miltiades (sixth to fifth century B.C.) was the Athenian general held responsible for the decision to fight (victoriously) the Persians at Marathon.

23 Plutarch, *Life of Themistocles*, Ch. 3: "It is said, indeed, that Themistocles was so carried away by his desire for reputation, and such an ambitious lover of great deeds, that though he was still a young man when the battle with the barbarians at Marathon was fought and the generalship of Miltiades was in everybody's mouth, he was seen thereafter to be wrapped in his own thoughts for the most part, and he was sleepless o' nights, and refused invitations to his customary drinking parties, and said to those who put wondering questions to him concerning his change

unchained itself in the long rivalry[24] with Aristides[25] up to that singularly noteworthy, purely instinctive genius of his political action, which Thucydides describes for us.[26] How characteristic the question and the answer is, if a noted opponent of Pericles is asked whether he or Pericles is the best wrestler in the city and gives the answer: "Even when I throw him down, he denies that he has fallen, he reaches his intention and persuades those who saw him fall."[27]

If one quite wants to see that feeling unveiled in its naïve expressions, the feeling of the necessity of the contest if the health of the state should endure, then one should think of the original sense of *ostracism*: as, e.g., the Ephesians express it with the exile of Hermador, "Among us no one should be the best: but if someone is it, then let him be elsewhere and with others."[28] For wherefore should no one be the best? Because thereby the contest would be exhausted and the eternal basis of life of the Hellenic state would be endangered. Later ostracism received another position with respect to the contest: it is employed when the danger is manifest [offenkundig] that one of the great ones from among the contesting politicians and party leaders feels enticed, in the heat of the battle, to harmful and destroying means and to dubi-

of life that the trophy of Miltiades would not suffer him to sleep." Bernodotte Perin, translator; Cambridge: Harvard University Press, 1959.

24 Plutarch portrays Themistocles and Aristides as long term opponents whose rivalry began in private over a lover and grew out into the public sphere (*Life of Themistocles*, Ch. 3).

25 Aristides (sixth to fifth century B.C.) was an Athenian politician and leading member of the aristocratic faction and opponent of Themistocles. He was sometimes referred to as "the just."

26 Thucydides, Book I, paragraphs 90–93.

27 Plutarch, *Life of Pericles*, Ch. 8.

28 Heraclitus, Fragment 121: ἄξιον Ἐφεσίοις ἡβηδὸν ἀπάγξασθαι πᾶσι καὶ τοῖς ἀνήβοις τὴν πόλιν καταλιπεῖν οἵτινες Ἑρμόδωρον ἄνδρα ἑωυτῶν ὀνήιστον ἐξέβαλον φάντες· ἡμέων μηδὲ εἷς ὀνήιστος ἔστω, εἰ δὲ μή, ἄλλη τε καὶ μετ᾽ ἄλλων. "All the Ephesians from youth upward deserve to be carried off to prison and to leave the city to those not yet come to manhood, for they threw out Hermodorus, the most advantaged man of them, saying, "There will be among us not even one most advantaged, but if such there be, [let him be] elsewhere and with others."

ous coups d'etats.[29] The original sense of this odd arrangement, however, is not that of a vent, rather that of a means of stimulation: one removes the over-towering individual, thereby now again the contest [Wettspiel] of forces awakes: a thought that is hostile to the "exclusivity" of genius in the modern sense, but which assumes that, in a natural order of things, there are always *more* geniuses who reciprocally incite [each other] to deeds, as they also reciprocally hold [each other] within the borders of measure. That is the kernel of the Hellenic contest-idea: it abhors solitary mastery and fears its dangers; it requires, as a *means of protection* against the genius – a second genius.

Every gift must unfold itself in fighting; thus commands the Hellenic, popular pedagogy: whereas the newer educators have in the face of nothing so great a shyness as in the face of the unchaining of so-called ambition. Here they fear self-seeking as "evil in itself" – with the exception of the Jesuits, who are therein minded like the ancients and therefore are enabled probably to be the most effective educators of our time. They appear to believe that self-seeking, i.e., the individual, is only the most powerful [kräftigste] agent, but its character as "good" and "evil" essentially comes from the goals after which it stretches out. But for the ancients the goal of the agonal education was the welfare of the whole, the state [staatlichen] society. Every Athenian, e.g., should develop himself in the contest so far as to be of the highest usefulness to Athens and to bring the least harm. There was no ambition up into the unmeasured and the not-to-be-measured as with most of modern ambition: the youth thought of the well-being of his mother city when he, for the sake of the contest, ran or threw or sang; he wanted to increase its fame in his own; he consecrated to his city's gods the garlands that the judges [Kampfrichter] reverently set upon his head. Every Greek felt in himself, from childhood on, the burning wish to be an instrument of the salvation of his city in the contest of the cities: therein was his self-seeking enflamed, therein was it reined in and closeted. Therefore the individuals in antiquity were freer, because their goals were closer and more graspable. The modern human being, on the contrary, is generally crossed by infinity like the

29 Nietzsche does not use French here, and I hope this phrase can be understood as ordinary English.

swift-footed Achilles in the parable of the Eleatic Zeno: infinity hems him in, he does not once catch up with the turtle.[30]

But just as the youths to be educated would be educated with one another by contesting, so were again their educators in a contest among themselves. Mistrusting-jealously, the great musical masters, Pindar[31] and Simonides,[32] strode forth next to one another; in a contesting manner the sophist, the higher teacher of antiquity, encountered other sophists; even the most general kind of instruction, through the drama, was only conferred on the people under the form of a monstrous wrestling match of the great musical and dramatic artists. How wonderful! "Even the artist resents [grollt] the artist!" And the modern human being fears nothing so much in an artist as the personal impulse to battle, whereas the Greek is familiar with the artist *only in the personal battle*. There where the modern human being smells the weakness of a work of art, the Hellene seeks the fount of its highest power [Kraft]! That, which, e.g., with Plato, is of special artistic significance in his dialogues, is mostly the result of a contest with the art of the

30 This refers to the one of Zeno's famous paradoxes of motion that deals with a race between Achilles and a turtle that is given a head start: "And there are four arguments of Zeno about motion, which give indigestion to those who unravel them. . . . Second is the so-called Achilles, and it is this: that the slowest running, will never be left behind by the fastest, since before that the pursuer must have come to the place the pursued set off from, so that the slower is necessarily always in front by some amount. But this is the same argument as the bisecting, but differs in that the dividing of the magnitude taken beforehand is not in half. The not catching up with the slower follows from the argument, but it comes about by means of the same thing as the bisecting (for in both, the magnitude being divided in some way, the not coming to the end follows, but in this one it is piled on that not even will the one represented as fastest in the tragedies do so in pursuing the slowest)" Aristotle, *Physics*, 239b10–25, Joe Sachs translator; New Brunswick, N.J.: Rutgers University Press, 1998.

31 Pindar was a lyric poet born about 518 B.C. and reputed to live for 81 years.

32 Simonides was a Greek poet born about 556 B.C. and reputed to live for 90 years. Pindar was held by some in antiquity to have attacked Simonides as a "Muse for hire;" see *Isthmian Odes*, II, line 6.

rhetors, the sophists, and the dramatists of his time, invented for the purpose that he at last could say: "Look, I can do that also, what my great rivals can do; indeed, I can do it better than they. No *Protagoras*[33] composed such beautiful myths as I, no dramatist such an animated and captivating [fesselndes][34] whole as the Symposium, no rhetor has authored such a speech as I put into the *Gorgias* – and now I reject that altogether and condemn all imitative art! Only the contest made me into a poet, into a sophist, into a rhetor!" What a problem opens itself to us there, when we ask after the relation of the contest to the conception of the work of art!

Let us take away, on the contrary, the contest form from Greek life, thus we see immediately in that pre-Homeric abyss a horrible wildness of hatred and lust to annihilate. This phenomenon shows itself unfortunately so frequently when a great personality was removed from a contest through a monstrously brilliant deed and was hors de concours[35] according to his own and to his fellow citizens' judgment. The effect is, almost without exception, an appalling [entsetzliche] one; and if one usually draws the conclusion from these effects that the Greek had been incapable of enduring [ertragen] fame and fortune [Glück]: thus one should speak more precisely that he was not able to bear [tragen] fame without further contest, fortune at the conclusion of a contest. There is no clearer example than the final destiny of Miltiades. Through an incomparable result at Marathon [he was] placed upon a singular peak and raised far beyond, above every fellow struggler: he feels in himself a low, revenge-seeking lust awake toward a citizen of Para with whom he had an enmity ages ago. In order to satisfy this lust he misuses his reputation, the state's power and civic honor, and dishonors himself. In a feeling of failure he falls into unworthy machinations. He enters into a secret and godless union with the priestess of Demeter, Timo, and at night trespasses in the holy temple from which every man was excluded. As he has sprung over the wall and comes ever nearer to the holiness of the goddess, suddenly the fearsome hor-

---

33 Protagoras of Abdera (c.490–420 B.C.) was the most famous of the sophists of the Greek world.
34 More literally, "chaining."
35 French for "outside of the concourse," meaning "with no possible rivals."

ror of a panicky terror falls over him: almost collapsing and without reflection [Besinnung] he feels himself driven back, and springing back over the wall, he tumbles down lamed [gelähmt] and badly hurt [schwer verletzt]. The siege had to be lifted, the people's court awaited him, and a disgraceful death presses its seal upon a brilliant hero's career, in order to darken it for all posterity.[36] After the battle at Marathon the envy of the heavenly ones seized on him. And this divine envy catches fire when it sees a human being without any contenders, without opponents, upon a singular height of fame. Only the gods does he now have next to him – and therefore he has them against him. But these seduce him to an act of hubris, and under it he collapses.

Let us mark well that as Miltiades perished, so perished the noblest Greek states as they, through service and fortune, had arrived from the race course at the temple of Nike. Athens, which had annihilated the independence of its allies and punished with rigor the revolts of the downtrodden [Unterworfenen], Sparta, which after the battle of Aegospotamoi[37] made hold its superiority over Hellas in still much harder and more cruel ways, have also, after the example of Miltiades, through acts of hubris brought about their perishing,[38] as a proof thereby that without envy, jealousy, and contesting ambition the Hellenic state, like the Hellenic human being, degenerates. It becomes evil and cruel; it becomes revenge-seeking and godless; in short, it becomes "pre-Homeric" – and then it merely requires a panicky terror in order to bring it to a fall and to smash it. Sparta and Athens surrender themselves to Persia, as Themistocles[39] and Alcibiades[40] had done; they betray the Hellenic after they had given up the noblest, Hellenic basic thought, the contest: and Alexander, that coarsened copy and abbreviation of Greek history, now invents the Hellene of the whole world [Allerwelts-Hellene] and so-called "Hellenism."

Ended on 29 December 1872

36 See Herodotus, *Histories*, Book VI. 133–136.
37 Naval defeat of Athens by Sparta in 405 B.C.; cf. Xenophon, *Hellenica*, Book II.10–32.
38 Or "decline."
39 See Thucydides, Book I, paragraphs 135–138.
40 See Thucydides, Book VIII, paragraphs 45 ff.

Appendix: Preliminary Drafts

This appendix consists of sixteen preliminary drafts or fragments of preliminary drafts of the five prefaces. Fifteen of these preliminary drafts can be found in the *Kritische Gesamtausgabe* division III, volume 5/1, pp. 821–847 in the Nachbericht, or "After commentary," to the third division of Nietzsche's collected works. They are taken from the pages of a number of different notebooks, and I have indicated in parentheses the critical editor's designations for the source notebook for each fragment, for example, (*U I* 6, 9–12.). The one exception is draft number seven, the preliminary draft of *The Greek State*. This draft, for whatever reason, does not appear in the Nachbericht. It covers the entire text of *The Greek State*, sandwiched between text not to be found in that essay. This draft belongs to a small notebook all its own, that Nietzsche labeled, "*Fragment of an Expanded Form of the 'Birth of Tragedy,'* written in the first weeks of the year 1871. 11 pages." It can be found in the *Kritische Gesamtausgabe* division III, volume 3, pp. 346–363. If one wishes to see a prelimary draft of *Thoughts on the Future of Our Educational Institutions*, see the *Preface* to *On the Future of Our Educational Institutions* (St. Augustine's Press, 2004).

There are many differences, some gross, many subtle, between these preliminary notes and the "final" form of the five prefaces. I have tried to represent these differences in my translation. Still, though I have cleaned up the text in a couple of instances, I have tried to make these notes look as they do in the critical editions, and thus I have left in oddities of paragraph indentation or lack thereof, or persistent and idiosyncratic use of colons, and I have represented Nietzsche's abbreviation u. of the conjunction und ("and") as the symbol "&." It is my hope that subtle readers can use this appendix as a significant aid to their own reading of Nietzsche. Small variations, the presence or absence of a key phrase, the decision to substitute one phrase or passage for another, even changes in word order or punctuation may help to enrich and inform the careful reader's interpretations of these prefatory and at times skeletal essays.

On the Pathos of Truth

1. Compare paragraphs 1–3. (*U I* 6, 9–12.)
Is fame really only the most delicious mouthful of our love of our own? – It is indeed tied to the rarest human beings, as a lust: and again to the rarest moments of the same. These are the moments of ingenious enlightenments, both with men of deeds as of art & of knowledge. I recognize as a fundamental form of fame the instinctive, sudden certainty, that that which raised us thus & whisked us away, thus the height of this *one* feeling should remain withheld from no posterity: in the eternal necessity of those rarest highest moments the human being feels the eternal necessity of his fame: humanity, into all of the future – needs us, i.e., it needs us in our highest moments – then namely are we wholly ourselves, everything else is dross, morass, vanity, passing away.

It is a fearsome thought, that a monstrous mountain sinks down – how we ourselves feel heavy heartedly the tumbling down of a tall tree. But that one moment of the highest world perfection as it were, without a posterity should disappear like a fleeting flash of light, offends most strongly of all the moral [sittlichen] human being. His imperative says much more: that which is eternally necessary, so that human beings are human beings, that must also be eternally present. This uninterrupted chain of great moments, this mountain range, binding itself through the millennia, we name culture. That for me the greatness of a past time is still great, that the anticipating belief of the one lusting for fame is fulfilled, but that is a task, the problem of culture, conditioned by the difficulty of its *tradition*.

There are indeed pitiful, short-living human beings, surrendered to their narrow needs, ever again awakening to the same necessities & with trouble saving themselves in the face of the same. How may one suppose, among them, that apparently luxurious cultivation and that highly difficult torch race through which greatness lives farther? Greatness! Carried farther in human intellects!

But [it] is no merely luxurious embalming of the going over, not only a historical collection of curiosities – rather the eternal *fruitfulness* of everything great declares the eternal neediness of the human being for [nach] this greatness. The noble deed catches fire in the noble deed – thus goes an electric chain from every great one through the millennia. Infinity & inexhaustibility is the essence of greatness – no time will use it up.

2. Compare paragraphs 1–6. (*MP XII* 4, 10–12.)

Is fame really only the most delicious mouthful of our love of our own? – It is indeed tied to the rarest human beings, as a lust, and again to the rarest moments of the same. These are the moments of sudden enlightenments, in which a human being stretches out his arm, as if toward a world creation, commanding, drawing light out of himself and streaming out around him. Here the happy-making certainty permeates him that that which raised him even thus out into the most distant and whisked him away, thus the height of this one feeling, should remain withheld from no posterity; in the eternal necessity of those rarest enlightenments for all who are coming, the human being recognizes the necessity of his fame; humanity, right into all of the future, needs him, and as that moment of enlightenment is the epitome [Auszug] and totality [Inbegriff] of his ownmost essence, thus he believes himself, as the human being of this moment, to be undying, whereas he throws everything else from himself as dross, vanity, animality, or as pleonasm and surrenders them to passing away.

Every disappearing we see with dissatisfaction: a tall tree collapses to our displeasure and tortures us. But that one instance of the highest world perfection as it were, without a posterity, should disappear like a fleeting flash of light, offends most strongly of all the moral [sit-tlichen] human being. His imperative says much more: that which was *once* there, in order more beautifully to propagate the concept "human being," that must also be eternally present. That the great moments form a chain, that they bind a mountain range of humanity through the millennia, that for me the greatness of a past time is also great and that the anticipating belief of the one lusting for fame is fulfilled, that is the fundamental thought of *culture* [Kultur].

In response to the demand that greatness should be eternal, the fearful battle of culture [Kultur] bursts into flames; for everything else that still lives calls out No! The usual, the small, the common, filling all corners of the world, like heavy earthly air which we all are con-demned to breathe, making smoke around the greatness, obstructing, dampening, suffocating, making muddy, deceiving, throw themselves into the way that greatness has to go toward immortality. The way leads through human brains! Through the brains of pitiful, short-living ones surrendered to their narrow needs, ever again to the same neces-sities and with trouble warding destruction off from themselves for a short time. They want to live, to live somewhat – at any price! Who may suppose, among them, that difficult torch-race through which alone greatness lives further? And indeed a few awaken ever again who feel themselves so blessed with a view to that greatness as if human life were a masterly thing and as if the most beautiful fruit of this bitter plant were to know, that once someone proud and stoic has gone through this existence, another with profundity [Tiefsinn],[1] a third with pity [Erbarmen], but all leaving behind one teaching, that whoever lives existence most beautifully, that one does not respect it. If the common human being takes this span of being so gloomily [trüb-sinnig] seriously, those knew upon their journey toward immortality how to bring it to an Olympian laughing or at least to an elevating [erhabenen][2] disdain [Hohne]: often they climb with irony into their grave – for what [was] in them to be entombed [begraben]?

The boldest companions among these fame seekers must, howev-er, be the great philosophers. Their effects are not pointed at a "pub-

1   This could also mean "melancholy."
2   Or "sublime."

likum,"[3] at the approval of the masses and the shouting [zujauchzenden] chorus of contemporaries; to march [ziehn] the street alone belongs to their essence. Their gift is the rarest and even the most excluding and most hostile against gifts of the same kind. The wall of their self-sufficiency must be of diamond, if it should not be ruined and broken, for everything is in movement against them. Their journey toward immortality is more difficult and more hindered than any other: and yet no one upon [the journey] can expect [glauben] more securely than precisely the philosopher – to come to the goal, because he, as it were, does not know where he should stand if not upon the wide outstretched wings[4] of all times; for disrespect of the present and the momentary lies in the authentically philosophic manner [Art] of his consideration [Betrachtung]. He has the truth; the wheel of time may roll whereto it wants; it will never be able to flee from the truth.

It is important to experience of such human beings that they once had lived. One would never be able to imagine as an idle possibility the pride of the wise Heraclitus, who may be our example. In itself indeed every striving after knowledge, according to its essence, appears unsatisfied and unsatisfying: therefore no one, if he has not been instructed by history, will be able to believe in such a kingly self-respect, and state of conviction that one is the made-happy [beglückte] suitor of the truth. Such human beings live in their own solar system: therein one must seek them out. Even a Pythagoras, an Empedocles treated himself with a superhuman esteem, indeed with almost religious shyness, but the bond of sympathy, tied to the great conviction of transmigration of souls and the unity of everything living, led them again to other human beings, to their salvation. But of the feeling of loneliness that permeated the Ephesian hermit,[5] one can only sense something while growing cold in the wildest mountain waste. No overpowering feeling of sympathetic excitements, no desires to want to help and save, stream out from him. His eye, flaming, directed toward the inside, looks dead and icy, toward the outside. All around him, waves of madness [Wahns] and absurdity [Verkehrtheit] beat immediately on the fastness

3   Latin for "public."
4   Reading Fittiche for Fittigen.
5   See footnote 14 of *Pathos*.

of his pride: with disgust he turns away from them. But even human beings with feeling breasts avoid such an iron mask [Larve]: in a cast-off holiness, among images of gods, cold, grand architecture such a being [Wesen] may appear more conceivable. Among human beings Heraclitus was unbelievable: he did not need human beings, not even for his knowledge; there lay nothing for him in everything which one could possibly ask of them. "I sought and investigated myself,"[6] he said of himself with a phrase [Worte] by which one designated the investigation of an oracle: the fulfiller & completer of that Delphic principle (knw. yrslf.).

But what he [had] from this oracle, he held for immortal as the prophetic speeches of the Sibyl are. It is enough for the most distant humanity: may they[7] what he, like the Delphic god, "neither says, nor conceals."[8] Similarly, if it is proclaimed by him "without laughing, without finery and scented ointment," much more as "with foaming mouth," it must penetrate thousands of years into the future.[9] For the world needs eternally the truth; thus it needs eternally Heraclitus, although he does not require it. What does his fame matter to him! Fame with mortals,[10] as he mockingly exclaimed. That is something for singers and poets, also for those who had been known before him as "wise" men: these may gobble up the most delicious morsel of love of their own; for him this meal is too common. His fame matters somewhat to human beings, not to him; his love of his own is the love of truth – and this truth says to him that the immortality of humanity needs him, not that he needs the immortality of the human being. But from him humanity has the doctrine[11] of "Law in becoming," the fundamental dogma of all natural science.[12]

6   See footnote 17 of *Pathos*.
7   Some thought seems to need to be supplied here.
8   See footnote 19 of *Pathos*.
9   See footnote 20 of *Pathos*.
10   See footnote 21 of *Pathos*.
11   Or, "teaching."
12   More literally, "natural research."

3. Compare paragraphs 4 – 6. (*P I* 20, 118–119.)

The boldest companions among these must, however, be the great philosophers: their effects are not pointed at agreement[13] of the masses, at the jubilating chorus of contemporaries, to march [ziehn] the street alone belongs to their essence. Their gift is the rarest, thereby most excluding & most hostile against everything similarly gifted. The wall of their self-sufficiency must be of diamond, if it should not be ruined & broken; for everything is in movement against them. Their journey toward immortality is difficult but no one upon [it is] more secure than the philosopher to reach this goal, because he, as it were, does not know where he should stand if not upon the wide out-stretched wings[14] of all times; indeed disrespect of the present lies locked into his authentically philosophic [nature].[15] He has the truth: the wheel of time may roll whereto it wants; it will never be able to flee from the truth. It is important to experience of such human beings that they once had lived: one would never be able to imagine as an idle possibility the pride of Heraclitus, who may be our example. In itself indeed every striving after knowledge according to its essence [is] unsatisfied: therefore no one will be able to believe in such a kingly self-respect & conviction to have found the truth if he is not instructed by history that there was a Heraclitus. Even a Pythagoras, an Empedocles treated himself with a superhuman esteem, indeed with almost religious dignity,[16] but the bond of sympathy, tied to the great conviction of transmigration of souls & the unity of everything living, led them again to other human beings, to their salvation. But of the feeling of loneliness that permeated the Ephesian hermit,[17] one can only sense something while growing cold: no overpowering feeling of sympathetic emotions [Regungen], no desires to want to help & use, stream out from him. All around him waves of blind madness [Wahns], of absurdity [Verkehrtheit], beat now immediately on the fastness of his pride: with disgust he shies away from them. Such a human being

13 Reading Beistimmung for the fragmentary "eistimm."
14 Reading Fittiche for Fittigen.
15 "Nature" is just a suggestion here. Some noun needs to be supplied.
16 Or, "worth."
17 See footnote 14 of *Pathos*.

with the iron mask [Larve] must one represent in the cast-off holiness, among images of gods, among human beings he was unbelievable and most importantly [höchstens] he could once entertain[18] himself playing with children. He did not need human beings, not even for his knowledge: there lay nothing for him in everything which one could ask of them. "I sought and investigated myself,"[19] he spoke of himself with a phrase [Worte] by which one designated the investigation of an oracle. But what he [had] from this one he held for immortal, as the speeches of wisdom of the Sibyl are immortal: similarly, if it were noted of him "without laughing, without finery & scented ointment," it must speak thousands of years to posterity.[20] For the world needs eternally the truth; thus it needs eternally Heraclitus, although he does not require it. Here climbs up that problem before him that the historicizing educated one [Gebildete] and the complacent Philistine beat back from themselves with all the force [Kraft] of their instinct, the problem, from which there is no refuge, "the rational development."

4. Compare paragraph 11. (*P I* 20, 152.)

In some remote corner of the universe filled up with countless solar systems twinkling there was once a star [Gestirn][21] on which clever animals invented *knowledge*. It was the most arrogant [hochmüthigste] and most lying minute of "world history": after a few courses of the breath of nature the star grew cold, the clever animals die. In time: for if they already "knew," they had indeed finally come behind [the fact] that they had known everything falsely. They died and cursed the truth. That was the way [Art] of these desperate animals, who had discovered knowledge.

5. Compare paragraph 12. (*P I* 20, 130.)

This were the lot of the human being if it were just only a knowing animal. Truth would drive it to despair and to annihilation. To the human being is fitting not the truth, rather the belief in the truth, i.e., the trustful illusion.

18   Reading ergötzen for ergetzen.
19   See footnote 17 of *Pathos*.
20   See footnote 20 of *Pathos*.
21   This was translated earlier as "constellation."

6. Compare paragraphs 12 and 13. (*P I* 20, 130–131.)

Does he not live in a continuous becoming deceived? Does not nature conceal from him most things [Allermeiste], in order to banish him & lock him into a fantastic illusionist's [gauklerisches] "consciousness"? It threw away the key & woe to the poor one, who would like for once to look out & down through a crack out of the room of consciousness & who knew how the "human being" rests upon the pitiless, the disgusting, the greedy, the insatiable, the murderous, in the indifference of his not knowing &, as it were, hanging upon the back of a tiger in dreams.

Let him hang, calls art. Wake him up, calls the philosopher; he himself sinks down into a still deeper slumber, in which he dreams of truth & of immortality. Art is more powerful than knowledge, for the former wants life & the latter going under [Untergang].

The Greek State

7. Compare the entire essay.

Now to whomever has been disclosed, through the characterization given up till now, the sense for both the opposed and yet belonging together worlds of the Apollinian and of the Dionysian, he will go now one step further and, from out of the standpoint of that knowledge, grasp *the Hellenic life* in its most important manifestations [Erscheinungen] as a *preparation* for the highest expressions [Äußerungen] of those drives *for the birth of genius*. Whereas we ourselves must think of namely those drives *as forces of nature* outside of all connection with social, state, religious orders and mores [Sitten], there is still a more artistic and superiorly prepared, almost indirect revelation of those drives, through the individual *genius*, about whose nature and highest significance I must now permit myself a half mystical speech full of images [Bilderrede].

The *human being* and the *genius* stand over against each other insofar as the first is throughout a work of art, without himself being conscious of that, because the satisfaction in him as in a work of art belongs wholly to another species of knowledge and consideration:[22] in this sense he belongs to nature, which is nothing except a mirroring, courteous to vision, of the original-unity [Ur-Eine]. In the genius on the contrary is – outside of the significance coming to him as a human being – at the same time still that authentic power [Kraft] of another sphere, to feel himself the ecstasy of vision, present. If the satisfaction in dreaming human beings discloses itself to him only in a dawning fashion [dämmernd], at the same time the genius is capable of the highest satisfaction in this circumstance; as he himself has on the other side force over this circumstance and can produce it out of himself alone. After that, what we have remarked about the predominating significance of the dream for the original-unity, we may look at the collected *waking* life of the individual human being as a preparation for his dreams; now we must add to this, that *the collected dream life of many human beings* on the other hand is the preparation of the *genius*. In this world of not-being, everything must *become* out of appearance: and thus will even the genius, in that in one complex of humanity, in one great individual that dawning [dämmernde] feeling of the pleasure of the dream itself climbs ever more, up to that genius, the authentic delight: which phenomenon we can make visible to ourselves in the gradually heralded rising of the sun, through the rosy morning [Morgenröthe] and the rays sent out before. Humanity, with all nature as its to-be-supposed mother's lap, may be designated in this furthest sense as the continual birth of the genius: from out of that monstrous omnipresent viewpoint of the original-unity the genius is reached in every moment, the whole pyramid of appearance up to its peak is completed. We, in the narrowness of our view and within the representational mechanism of time, space, and causality, have to resign ourselves, when we recognize the genius as one among many and after many human beings; indeed we may be fortunate [glücklich] if we have generally recognized him, which at bottom can ever happen only accidentally and in many cases certainly has never happened.

The genius as the "not waking and only dreaming" human being, who, as I said, is prepared and emerges in the human being at the same

22 Or "observation."

time waking and dreaming, is through and through an *Apollinian* nature: a truth, that, after the aforementioned characterization of the Apollinian, makes itself clear. With that we will be pressed toward a definition of the *Dionysian* genius, as of the human being become one, in full self-forgetting, with the original ground [Urgrunde] of the world, who now from out of the original pain [Urschmerze] creates a counter-appearance to the same to his redemption: how we have to revere this process in the *saint* and the great *musician*; both are only repetitions of the world and second castings of the same.

When this artistic reappearance [Wiederschein] of the original pain [Urschmerzes] from out of itself produces yet a second mirroring, as a parhelion:[23] thus we have the common *Dionysian-Apollinian* art work, whose mystery we seek to approach in this speech full of images.

For that one world-eye, before which the empirically-real world *altogether*[24] pours out its reappearance [Wiederscheine] into the dream, thus that Dionysian-Apollinian unification is an eternal and unalterable, indeed singular form of delight: there is no Dionysian appearance [Schein] without an Apollinian reappearance [Wiederschein]. For our short-sighted eye, almost gone blind, that phenomenon lies apart in pure individual delight, part Apollinian, part Dionysian, and only in the art work[25] of tragedy do we hear that highest double art speaking to us, which, in its unification of the Apollinian and the Dionysian is the copy of that original delight of the world-eye. Just as for this one the genius is the peak of the pyramid of appearance, so may we, on the other hand, hold the tragic artwork as the peak of the artistic pyramid reachable for our eye.

We, who are obliged,[26] to understand everything under the form of becoming, i.e., as *willing*, pursue now the *birth* of the three different kinds of geniuses into the world of appearance familiar to us alone: we investigate which most important *preparations* the "will" needs [braucht], in order to acquire them. Therewith we have all grounds, to give this account [Nachweis] of the Greek world, which speaks to us about that process simply and expressively, as is its manner.

23   Parhelion means "alongside the sun."
24   Or "collected," reading samt for sammt.
25   Or "artistic effect."
26   Or "compelled."

In the case that the genius really is the target goal [Zielpunkt] and final intention of nature, thus must it now also be provable [nachweisbar] that, in the other forms of appearance of the Hellenic essence [Wesen], only necessary helping mechanisms and preparations for that final goal are to be recognized. This viewpoint compels us to investigate down to their roots much referred to conditions of antiquity, about which still no modern[27] human being has spoken with sympathy: whereby it will emerge [ergeben], that these roots are exactly that out of which the wonderful tree of life of Greek art could solely spring. It may be that this knowledge fills us with shuddering: yet this shuddering belongs almost to the necessary effects of every deeper knowledge. For nature is even somewhat terrible, where she is strained to create the most beautiful thing. To this one it is appropriate to its essence, that the triumphal procession of *culture* [Kultur] comes to good only for an unbelievably small minority of privileged mortals, that against that, the *slavish servitude* of the great masses is a necessity, if it really should come to a proper pleasure in the process [Werdelust] of art.[28] We moderns[29] have an advantage over the Greeks in two concepts, spreading themselves out peacock-like, which as it were have been given as a means of consolation to a world comporting itself slavishly throughout and at the same time anxiously shying away from the word "slave": we speak of the dignity [Würde] of the human being and of the "dignity of work." Everything tortures in order miserably to perpetuate a miserable life; this fearful necessity compels toward consuming work, which now the human being seduced by the "will" casually [gelegentlich] stares at as something full of dignity. But so that work would earn honor and laudable [rühmliche] names, it would be necessary before everything that existence itself, for which it is indeed only a tortuous means, have somewhat more dignity than this is accustomed to manifest [erscheinen] to seriously intended philosophies and religions. What else may we find in the necessity to work of all the millions than the drive to vegetate further at any price, and who does not see in

27 More literally, "newer."
28 Starting here the text constitutes a variant on the entire essay, *The Greek State*.
29 More literally, "newer ones."

stunted plants that stretch their roots into soilless stone, the same all-powerful drive?

Out of this dreadful struggle for existence can pop up only the individuals who now immediately again will be preoccupied by the illusory images of an artistic culture [Kultur], so that they do not only come to the practical pessimism: as that circumstance which nature abhors in the highest degree. In the modern[30] world, which, over against the Greek one, most of all creates abnormalities and centaurs, in which the individual human being, like that fabulous being at the beginning of Horace's Poetics,[31] is colorfully put together out of pieces, the lust of the struggle for existence and the need for art shows itself often at the same time in the same human being: out of which unnatural melting together the necessity has emerged to excuse and to some extent to consecrate that first lust before the need for art, which has happened through that exquisite idea [Vorstellung] of the dignity of the human being and of work. The Greeks need no such lamentable makeshifts,[32] with them it is expressed purely that work is a disgrace – not as it were because existence [Dasein] is a disgrace, rather in the feeling of the impossibility that the human being struggling for the sake of naked survival could be an artist. The human being *in need of* art rules in antiquity, with his concepts, whereas in modern times,[33] the *slave* determines the ideas: he who, according to his nature, must designate all his circumstances[34] with deceptive, shining[35] names in order to be able to live. Such phantoms, as the dignity of the human being, the dignity of work, are the needy products of a slavish condition hiding from itself. Unblessed time, in which the slave has been stirred to reflection on himself and out above himself [über sich und über sich hinaus]! Unblessed seducer who has annihilated the innocent position of the slave through the fruit of the tree of knowledge! Now this one must, in order merely to be able to live, hold out with such transparent lies as

30 More literally, "newer."
31 See footnote 4 of *Greek State*.
32 More literally, "helps of necessity."
33 More literally, "the newer time."
34 Or "relations."
35 Glänzenden is translated elsewhere as "brilliant."

are recognizable for anyone looking more deeply into the alleged "equal rights of all," into the "basic rights of the human being," of the human being as species being, into the dignity of work. Indeed they are not permitted to conceive at what point, upon what level, "dignity" first, roughly can be spoken of – and the Greeks did not once allow it itself there – namely there where the individual fully surpasses himself and no longer must produce[36] and work in the service of his individual continued living. Even still upon this height of "work" the Greeks have the same deception-free naiveté. Even still that broken-off epigone, Plutarch, has so much Greek instinct in him, that he can say to us, no nobly born youth will have the longing if he looks at the Zeus in Pisa, to become himself a Phidias,[37] or if he sees the Hera in Argos to become himself a Polyklet:[38] and just as little would he harbor the wish to be Anacreon, Philetas, or Archilochus,[39] however much he even delights[40] in their poetries. Artistic creating falls for the Greeks just so much under the non-respect-worthy concept of work, like every banausic[41] handicraft. But if the compelling force of the artistic drive works in him, then he *must* create and subject himself to that necessity of work. And as a father admires the beauty and talent of his child, but thinks of the act of his birth [Entstehung] with shameful aversion, thus it goes with the Greek. The delightful marveling [Staunen] at the beautiful has not blinded him about the process of becoming, that appears to him like all creating in nature, as a violent necessity, as a greedy pressing-itself into existence. The same feeling, with which the process of procreation[42] is considered as something shameful to be hidden, although in it the human being serves a higher goal than his individual preservation: the same feeling fogs up around [umschleierte] even the birth [Entstehung] of the great work of art, despite the fact that through it a higher form of existence is inaugurated, as through that act a new generation is. *Shame* appears right authentically, conse-

36 Or "procreate."
37 See footnote 10 of *Greek State*.
38 See footnote 11 of *Greek State*.
39 See footnote 12 of *Greek State*.
40 Here Nietzsche has "ergötze."
41 See footnote 14 of *Greek State*.
42 Or "production."

quently to enter in there where the human being is still only a tool of unendingly greater appearances of will than he may value [gelten] himself in the singular form of the individual.

Now we have the general concept under which the feelings that the Greeks harbored in regard to slavery and to work are to be ordered. They held both as a necessary disgrace, in the face of which one feels shame: in this feeling the unconscious knowledge hides from itself that the authentic goal *needs* these presuppositions, but that here lies the horrible [Entsetztliche] and the bestial of the Sphinx nature, which in the deliberate glorification of the artistic, free life of culture [Kulturleben] stretches forth such a beautiful young woman's body. Culture [Bildung], which I understand as the true requirement of art, has a terrifying [erschrecklichen] substrate [Untergrund]: but this gives itself to be recognized in the dawning [dämmernde] feeling of shame. So that the soil [Erdboden] for a greater development of art is present, the monstrous majority, in the service of a minority, must be slavishly subjected to life's necessities *above* and beyond their individual requirements.[43] At its expense, through its working more, that favored class is supposed to be whisked away from the struggle for existence, in order now to produce a new world of requirements. According to this we must therefore understand, as a cruel fundamental condition of culture [Bildung] to be put down, that slavery belongs to the essence of a culture [Kultur]: knowledge which can produce already an appropriate shudder in the face of existence [Dasein]. These are the vultures that gnaw upon the liver of the Promethean promoter of culture. The misery of the human being living with difficulty must still be increased, in order to make possible the production of a world of art for a number of Olympian human beings. Here lies the source of that badly concealed wrath, which the communists and socialists and also their paler derivatives, the white race of liberals of every time, have nurtured against the arts, but also against classical antiquity. If culture [Kultur] really were granted to the discretion of a people, if inescapable powers did not rule here, which are law and limit to the individual, thus the contempt [Verachtung] of culture [Kultur], the glorification of poverty of spirit, the iconoclastic annihilation of artistic

43 Or "needs."

claims would be more than the revolt of the downtrodden [unterdrück-ten] masses against the dronelike individuals: it would be the cry of *pity*, which pulls down the walls of culture [Kultur]; the drive after equity, after an equal measure of suffering, would overflow into all other ideas. Really the excessive feeling of pity has at times for a short while, here and there, broken through all the dams of the cultural life [Kulturlebens]: a rainbow of pitying love and of peace appeared with the first stepping forth of Christendom, and under it was born its most beautiful fruit, the evangel of John. But there are also examples that powerful [mächtige] religions petrify to some extent a certain degree of culture [Kulturgrad] over long periods of time; think of the mum-mified thousand-year-old culture [Kultur] of the Egyptians. But one thing is not to be forgotten: this same cruelty, which we find in the essence of every culture [Kultur], lies also in the essence of every pow-erful [mächtige] religion; so that we will understand it well just as much if a culture [Kultur] with a cry for equity breaks down an all-too-high-towering bulwark of religious demands. Whatever wants to live, i.e., must live, in this terrible constellation of things, is at the bottom [Grunde] of its essence a portrait of the original pain [Urschmerzes] and of the original contradiction [Urwiderspruches], thus must fall into our eyes as "organs in accord with the world and the earth,"[44] as will, as insatiable lust for existence. Therefore we may even compare the glorious[45] culture with a victor dripping with blood, who in his tri-umphal procession drags along the conquered ones chained to his wagon as slaves: at which a charitable power has blinded their eyes, so that they, almost crushed by the wheels of the wagon, yet still call out "the dignity of work!" "the dignity of the human being!"

The modern human being to be sure is accustomed to a wholly other, softened consideration [Betrachtung] of things. For that reason he is eternally unsatisfied, because he never dares completely to trust himself to the fearsome, icily driving stream of existence [Dasein]; rather, he runs up and down anxiously on the bank. The modern[46] time with its "break" is to be conceived as fleeing backward in the face of

44 See footnote 19 of *Greek State*.
45 More literally, "lordly."
46 More literally, "newer."

all consequences: it wants to have nothing wholly, also [wants to have] wholly [nothing to do] with all of the natural cruelties of things. The dance of its thinking and driving is truly laughable, because it always hurls itself longingly upon new forms, in order to embrace them and then suddenly must let them go shuddering like Mephistopheles with the seductive Lamiae.[47] Out of the softening of the modern[48] human being are born the conditions of monstrous social need of the present, as whose antidote,[49] lying in the essence of nature, I dare to recommend *slavery*, slavery which neither original Christendom nor Germandom thought in any way objectionable, to say nothing of being reprehensible. In order to be silent about the Greek slaves: how sublimely does the consideration of the medieval serf work upon us, with the internally strong and tender relations of right and of morals ordered toward the higher one, with the profound [tiefsinnig] enclosure of his narrow existence. How sublime—and how reproachful!

Whoever now cannot reflect about the configuration of *society* without melancholy, whoever has learned to conceive of it as the ongoing painful birth of those eximious[50] human beings of culture [Kulturmenschen], in whose service everything else must consume itself, that one will also no longer be deceived by that false glitter which the moderns[51] have spread over the origin and the significance of the *state*. Namely, what can the state signify to us if it is not the means with which to bring into motion just that sketched social process and to guarantee it in its unhindered continuance? The drive toward sociability in individual human beings may even still be so strong, [but] first the iron clasp of the state presses the great masses so into one another that now that chemical division of society, with its new,

47 Lamiae are spirits that thirst for flesh and blood and assume various shapes, especially the shapes of seductive young women; Nietzsche is alluding to a scene in Goethe's *Faust*; see Part II, lines 7235–7238, 7696–7790; especially 7769–7785, where the Lamiae tempt Mephistopheles until he tries to embrace them, then they change shape and flit away.
48 More literally, "newer."
49 More literally, "counter-means."
50 See footnote 23 of *Greek State*.
51 More literally, "newer ones."

pyramidal arrangement, *must* advance. But from where springs forth this sudden power [Macht] of the state, whose goal lies far forward above the discernment,[52] indeed above the egoism of the individual? How did the slave emerge, the blind mole of culture [Kultur]? The Greeks revealed it to us in their instincts regarding the relations of right between peoples, who, even in the ripest fullness of their civilization and humanity, did not cease to cry out with a voice of brass[53] such words as: "To the victor belongs the defeated,[54] with woman and child, goods and blood. Force[55] gives the first right; and there is no right that does not have force as its ground."[56]

Thus we see again with what pitiless rigidity nature, in order to come to society, forged that cruel tool, the state: namely those conquerors with the iron hand that are nothing other than the objectification of that designated instinct. In their indefinable greatness and power [Macht], the observer [Betrachter] scents [spurt] that they are only a means for an intention revealing itself in them and yet concealing itself from them. It is just as though a magic [magischer] will streamed out from them, so puzzlingly swiftly do the weaker powers [Kräfte] attach themselves to them, so wonderfully do they transform themselves, at the sudden swelling of that avalanche of force,[57] under the magic [Zauber] of that creative kernel, into an affinity up till now not present.

If we now see, forthwith, how little the downtrodden ones concerned themselves about the terrifying origin of the state, so that at bottom about no kind of event does world history report worse to us than about the coming into being of the state of affairs of these violent [gewaltsamen], bloody, and almost always inexplicable usurpations: much more, if many more hearts involuntarily swell toward that magic [Magie] of the state, with the presentiment of an invisible deep intention, there where the calculating understanding is capable of seeing

52 More literally, "insight."
53 Or "brazen voice."
54 Or "victim."
55 Or "violence."
56 Or "act of violence."
57 Or "violence."

only an addition of powers [Kräfte]: if now, what is more, the state is considered [betrachtet] with ardor as the goal and peak of the sacrifices[58] and duties of the individual: thus all this expresses the monstrous necessity of the state, without which nature should not succeed to come through society to its redemption in appearance, in the mirror of the genius. What kind of knowledge does the instinctive pleasure in the state not overcome! One should indeed think that a being that looks into the emergence of the state, in the future would seek his salvation [Heil] only at a shuddersome distance from it: and where can one not see the memorials of that emergence, wasted lands, destroyed cities, human beings become wild, consuming hatred of peoples! The state, of disgraceful birth, for most beings a continually flowing fountain[59] of hardship, in frequently recurring periods the devouring torch of the human race – and nevertheless a sound, at which we forget ourselves, a call to battle that has inspired to countless truly heroic deeds, perhaps the highest, most worthy of respect for the blind and egoistic mass, which also has the strange expression of greatness upon its face only in the monstrous moments in the life of the state!

But we have to construe the Greeks, with a view to the singular solar altitude of their art, already a priori[60] as the "political human beings as such": and really history knows no second example of such a fearsome unchaining of the political drive, of such an unconditional sacrifice [Hinopferung] of all other interests in the service of this instinct for the state: at best [höchstens] one could in a comparative manner and from similar grounds honor [auszeichnen] the human beings of the Renaissance in Italy with a similar title. That drive is so overcharged with the Greeks that it begins ever again afresh [von neuem] to rage against itself and sink its teeth into its own flesh. This bloody jealousy of city toward city, of party toward party, this murderous lust of those small wars, the tigerish triumph over the corpse of the killed enemy, in short that incessant renewal of those Trojan scenes of war and atrocity, into which viewpoint Homer stands before us fully, *pleasurably* immersed, the typical Hellene – to where does this naïve

58 More literally, "offerings."
59 Or "source."
60 Latin for "from what is before."

barbarity of the Greek state point, from where does it take its excuse before the tribunal[61] of eternal justice?[62] Proudly and calmly the state stands before it: and it leads by the hand the gloriously blooming woman, Greek *society*. For this Helen it conducted those wars: what judge could condemn here?[63]

With this mysterious [geheimnißvoll] connection that we divine here between the state and art, political lust and artistic procreation, battlefield and art work, we understand by the state, as has been said, only the iron clasp that compels the social process: whereas without the state, in a natural bellum omnium contra omnes,[64] society generally cannot take root in a greater measure and out beyond the domain of the family. Now, after the universally entered-into formation of states, that drive of the bellum omnium contra omnes concentrates itself now of course into the horrifying thunderstorms of peoples and discharges itself, as it were, in rarer but so much stronger blows. But, in the pauses in between, society is yet allowed the time within which, according to the inwardly turned, pressed-together effect of that bellum, to germinate and to turn green all regions, in order to allow, as soon as there are a few warm days, the shining blooms of the genius to sprout forth.

In the face of the political world of the Hellenes I do not want to conceal in which appearances of the present I believe I recognize dangerous atrophies of the political sphere, equally precarious for art and society. If there should be human beings, which by birth, as it were, were placed outside of the instincts of peoples and states, which thus had to allow the state to be valid only so far as they conceived it to be in their own interests: thus shall human beings of such a kind necessarily represent to themselves as the final goal of the state the greatest possible undisturbed living next to one another of great political communities, in which they before all would be allowed to pursue their own intentions without limitation. With this representation in the head, they shall promote the politics that offers these intentions the greatest security, whereas it is unthinkable that they, against their intentions,

61 More literally, "judge's seat."
62 Gerechigkeit is translated elsewhere as "equity."
63 See footnote 35 of *Greek State*.
64 See footnote 36 of *Greek State*.

perhaps led by an unconscious instinct, should bring themselves to a sacrifice for the tendency of the state, unthinkable because they lack just that instinct. All other citizens of the state are, regarding what nature intends for them with their instincts for the state, in the dark and follow blindly; only those standing outside of this instinct know what they want from the state and what the state is supposed to guarantee them. Therefore it is precisely inevitable that such human beings gain a great influence over the state, because they are allowed to consider [betrachten] it as a *means*, whereas all others are, under the power [Macht] of the unconscious intentions of the state, themselves only means for the purposes of the state. In order now, through the means of the state, to reach the highest furtherance of their goals, useful to themselves, before everything it is necessary that the state will be completely freed from those terrible, incalculable convulsions of war, with that it can be used rationally; and with that they strive, as consciously as possible, for a state of affairs in which war is an impossibility. On this score, it is now held as valuable to curtail and to weaken as much as possible the special political drive and through the manufacture of great state bodies of *similar weight* and reciprocal guarantees of security [Sicherstellung] by the same to make the favorable result of an offensive war, and with that war generally, improbable in the highest degree; while they on the other hand[65] seek to wrest the question of war and peace away from the decision of individual possessors of power [Machthaber], in order to be able to appeal much more to the egoism of the mass or its representatives: whereto they in turn have the need to dissolve slowly the monarchic instincts of the people. They correspond to this purpose through the most universal diffusion of the liberal-optimistic world view, which has its roots in the teaching of the French Enlightenment and Revolution, i.e., in a wholly un-Germanic, *genuinely Romanic,* superficial[66] philosophy. I cannot help seeing before everything the effects of fear of war in the presently ruling movement of nationalities and the simultaneous diffusion of the universal right to vote; indeed in the background of these movements, as the genuinely fearing ones, I spot those truly international, homeless

65 More literally, "on the other side."
66 Or "flat."

financial hermits, who, with their natural lack of instinct for the state, have learned to misuse politics as a means of exchange and the state just as society as an apparatus for their own enrichment. Against the diversion, to be feared on this side, of the tendency of the state toward the tendency of money the single counter-means is war and war again: in whose excitation at least, still so much becomes clear, that the state was not founded upon the fear of the demon of war as the institution of protection of the egoistic individual, rather in the love of the father-land and of princes it produces out of itself an ethical impulse [Schwung] that refers to a much higher determination. If I thus desig-nate as a dangerous characteristic of the political present the employ-ment of thoughts of revolution in the service of a self-seeking [eigen-süchtigen], stateless aristocracy of money, if I conceive the monstrous diffusion of liberal optimism at the same time as the result of the mod-ern [modernen] money economy fallen into peculiar hands and see all the evils [Übel] of the social conditions [Zustände], including the nec-essary decline [Verfall] of the arts, either germinating out of that root or grown together with it: thus one will have to consider it good for me to occasionally strike up a paean to *war*. His silver bow resounds fear-somely: and if he comes at once here like the night, thus he is yet Apollo, the just [rechte][67] god of the consecration [Weihe] and purifi-cation of the state. But first, as it says in the beginning of the *Iliad*, he speeds the arrow at the mules and dogs. Then he even strikes human beings, and all over the woodpiles blaze with corpses.[68] So let it then be expressed that war is just such a necessity for the state, as the slave [is] for society: and who would be able to withhold[69] these findings[70] from himself, if he asks himself honestly about the grounds of the unreached perfection[71] of Greek art?

Whoever considers [betrachtet] war and its uniformed potentiality, the soldier class, with reference to the essence of the state portrayed so far, must come to the insight, that through war and in the soldier class

67 Or "proper."
68 See footnote 40 of *Greek State*.
69 More literally, "withdraw."
70 More literally, "knowledges."
71 Or "completion."

a copy [Abbild], indeed perhaps the original form [Urbild], of the state is placed before our eyes. Here we see, as a universal effect of the tendency of war, an immediate division and partition of the chaotic masses into military castes, from which in pyramidal form, with a broadest of all, slavish basis the edifice of a "warlike society" raises itself up. The unconscious purpose of the whole movement compels each individual under its yoke and produces[72] even in heterogeneous natures an almost chemical transformation of their properties, until they are brought into an affinity with that purpose. In the higher castes one scents already something more, about which it concerns itself at bottom with this inner process, namely the production[73] of the military genius – whom we have learned to recognize as the original founder of states. In many states, e.g., in Sparta's Lycurgan constitution,[74] one can clearly perceive the stamp of that fundamental idea of the state, the production of the military genius. Let us think now the original military state [Urstaat] in the most animated activity, in its authentic "work,"[75] and let us lead the whole practice [Technik][76] of war before our eyes; thus we cannot help to correct our concepts absorbed from all over, of the "dignity of work" and of the "dignity of the human being" by means of the question, whether the concept of dignity belongs[77] even then to the work which has as its purpose the annihilation [Vernichtung] of "dignified" human beings, whether the concept of "dignity" applies even to the human being who is entrusted with that "dignified work," or if not, whether, in this warlike task of the state, that concept, as one full of contradictions in itself, negates [aufheben] itself. I would have thought the warlike human being was a means of the military genius and his work, again, only a means of the same genius, and a degree of dignity comes to him not as an absolute human being and a non-genius; rather to him as a means of the genius – who can even choose his annihilation as a means of the warlike work of art

72 Or "procreates."
73 Or "procreation."
74 See footnote 46 of *Greek State*.
75 Or "task."
76 Or "technology."
77 More literally, "harmonizes."

– that dignity namely, to be considered worthy[78] to be the means of genius. What has been shown here in one singular example, holds in the most universal sense: every human being, with his collected activity, has only so much dignity as he, consciously or unconsciously, is a tool of the genius; from which the ethical consequence is immediately to be disclosed that the "human being in itself," the absolute human being, possesses neither dignity, nor rights, nor duties; only as a fully determined being serving unconscious purposes can a human being excuse his existence.

Plato's perfect[79] state is, according to these considerations [Betrachtungen], certainly still something greater than even the serious minded among its admirers[80] believe, not to speak at all of the smiling low estimation with which our "historically" educated know how to disapprove of such a fruit of antiquity. The authentic goal of the state, the Olympian existence and ever-renewed generation [Zeugung] of the genius, over against which all others are only preparatory means, is found here through a poetic intuition: Plato thoroughly saw through the terribly ravaged Herm[81] of the life of the state at that time and discerned even then still something divine in its inside.[82] He believed therein, that one could pull out this divine one and that the grim and barbaric distorted outside did not belong to the essence of the state; the whole ardor of his political passion stretched itself out after that wish. – That, in his perfect state, he did not place the genius in his universal concept at the peak, rather only the genius of wisdom assumed as the uppermost in the rank ordering, but generally shut the ingenious artist out of his state, that was a rigid consequence of the soon more closely-to-be-considered, Socratic judgment about art[83] which Plato, in a struggle against himself, had made into his own. This more external and nearly accidental omission may not be thoroughly reckoned among the main features of the Platonic state.

78 Gewürdigt is related to Würde, which has been translated throughout as "dignity."
79 Or "complete."
80 Or "reverencers."
81 See footnote 54 of *Greek State*.
82 See footnote 55 of *Greek State*.
83 See footnote 56 of *Greek State*.

As Plato dragged the innermost purpose of the state out of all of its coverings and murkiness into the light, thus he conceived also the deepest ground of the place of the *Hellenic woman* with respect to the state: in both cases he caught a glimpse in what was present around him, a copy of the ideas became revealed to him, before which to be sure the real was only a foggy image and play of shadows. Whoever, following after all-too-common habituation [Gewöhnung], holds generally the place of the Hellenic woman as unworthy and striving contrary to humanity, must themselves with this reproach turn even against the Platonic interpretation [Auffassung] of this place: for in it the present thing is only logically practiced [präcisirt]. Here thus our question repeats itself: should not the essence and the place of the Hellenic woman have a *necessary* reference to the target goal of the Hellenic will?

The most central thing[84] that Plato, as a Greek, could say about the place of the woman with respect to the state, was the so-offensive demand that in the perfect state the *family* must *cease*. Let us now foresee from that how he, in order to carry through this demand purely, even negated marriage and in its place festive [things], for the sake of the state − − − .

The Relation of Schopenhauerian Philosophy to a German Culture

8. Compare paragraph 1. (*P I* 20, 186.)
In dear lowly Germany culture [Bildung] now is so corrupt, envious looks [Scheelsucht] upon everything great stinking so up to heaven, and the general tumult of those running toward "happiness" so ear numbing, that one must have a strong belief, almost in the sense of credo quia absurdum est,[85] in order still to hope for a growing culture

84 More literally, "the innermost thing."
85 See footnote 1 of *Schopenhauer*.

[Kultur] and to work for the same – publicly instructing in opposition to the "public opinion" of the press. The undying concern with the people! We must therefore free ourselves from the momentary.

9. Compare paragraphs 1–3. (*U I* 4, 124–125.)

In dear lowly Germany culture [Bildung] now is so corrupt, envious looks [Scheelsucht] upon everything great stinking so up to heaven, and the general tumult of those running toward "happiness" so ear numbing, that one must have a strong belief, almost in the sense of credo quia absurdum est,[86] in order here indeed still to hope for a growing culture [Kultur] & before all else to be able to work for the same – publicly instructing in opposition to the "public opinion"[87] of the press. With force must they, those to whom the undying concern with the people lies at heart, free themselves from the impressions that storm at them of that which is present day [Gegenwärtigen] and to excite the appearance as if they reckoned these same things among the indifferent things: they must appear thus, because they want to think, & because a contrary view & a confounded one, probably indeed, disturbs their thinking with the trumpet blast of a sound mixed with the glory of war – but before all else, because they want to believe in that which is German & [to feel] in this belief their strength [Kraft]. These believing ones are not to be blamed if they very much from the distance and from above look down on the land of their promises! They shy away from the experiences that the well-wishing foreigner exposes, who now lives among Germans & wonders how little German life corresponds to those great individuals, works, & actions that he, in his well-wishing, had learned to revere as the authentically German. Whenever the German cannot elevate himself into the great he makes an impression as mediocre. Even the famous German science, in which a number of domestic and familial virtues, loyalty, purity, self-limitation, diligence, & modesty, appear transposed is still in no way the result of these virtues – driving toward unlimited knowledge looks like a lack, a defect, resembling much more a gap than a superfluity of strength [Kräften], almost like the result of a needy, formless, unlively

86 See footnote 1 of *Schopenhauer*.
87 More literally, "public opining."

life, & even like a flight from the small & the wicked, also, despite the science, indeed still within the science, breaks forth. Upon the limitation, in living & in knowing the Germans understand themselves as the true virtuosos of Philistinism – if one wants to carry them over themselves into the sublime,[88] thus they make themselves heavy like lead; whereas they are truly troubled to draw down their truly great ones out of the ether to themselves and to theirs by hung-on lead weights. Perhaps this Philistine-complacency is only the degeneration of a true [wahrhaft] German virtue, – a heartfelt sinking into the singular & the secret of the individual – but this moldy & degenerated virtue is now worse than the most obvious vice. The "cultured" [Gebildeten] of the well-known so cultivated [kultivirten] Germans, and the "Philistine*s*," among the well-known so uncultivated Germans, publicly shake hands & strike an agreement with one another, how henceforth one must write, paint, make music, in order neither to tread too distant from the "culture" [Bildung] of the one nor too closely to the complacency of the other. This, one now calls "The German Culture [Kultur] of the Present Day": whereby it would still only be to be asked by which specifications is that "cultured man" [Gebildete] [known], according to which his milk-brother, the German Philistine, gives himself now to be recognized. The "educated human being" [Gebildete] is now before all else historically educated [gebildet]; through his historical consciousness he saves himself in the face of the sublime,[89] the Philistine succeeds through his "complacency." No more the enthusiasm which history excites as indeed Goethe may have thought;[90] rather, the blunting [Abstumpfen] of all enthusiasm is now the goal of these admirers [Bewunderer] of the nil admirari,[91] when they seek to grasp [begreifen] everything historically; but one must call to them: "You are the fools of all centuries! History will only make confessions to you that are worthy of you! The world has been at all times full of trivialities, nothingnesses: your historical lusts [Gelüste] reveal themselves as just these and nothing else. You can by the thousands pounce upon an

88 Or, "the elevated."
89 Or, "the elevated."
90 See footnote 5 of *Schopenhauer*.
91 See footnote 6 of *Schopenhauer*.

epoch (– Illam ipsam quam jactant sanitatem non firmitate sed ieiunio consequuntur)[92] – Everything essential, it has not wanted to say to you, rather mocking & invisible it stood next to you, pressing into the hand of this one,[93] to that one a period [Jahneszahl], to a third an etymology. Do you really believe history can be reckoned up together like an addition problem, for which even the most common understanding were good enough? How must it annoy you to hear that others explain things, out of the most familiar times, that you will never and by no means grasp."

If now to this self-naming historical "culture" & to a philistinism hostile to & full of venom toward everything great yet that third cooperative [Genossenschaft] comes – those who run toward "happiness" – thus there will be in summa such a confounded outcry and such a limb-contorting throng that the thinker will flee into the loneliest wilderness with stopped-up ears & closed eyes – therein he may see what all those saw, may hear what resounds to him out of all the depths of nature and down from the stars – the eternal melody [Weise].[94]

10. Compare the entire essay. (*Mp XIII* 2, 6–8.)

In dear lowly Germany culture [Bildung] now is so corrupt, envious looks [Scheelsucht] upon everything great stinking so up to heaven, and the general tumult of those running toward "happiness" so ear numbing, that one must have a strong belief, almost in the sense of credo quia absurdum est,[95] in order here indeed still to hope for a growing culture [Kultur] and before all else to be able to work for the same – publicly instructing in opposition to the "public opinion"[96] of the press. With force must they, those to whom the undying concern with the people lies at heart, free themselves from the impressions that storm in upon them of that which is precisely now present day [Gegenwärtigen] and current [Geltenden] and to excite the appearance as if they reckoned these same things among the indifferent things.

92 See footnote 7 of *Schopenhauer*.
93 Some subject or task has to be supplied here.
94 Or, "way."
95 See footnote 1 of *Schopenhauer*.
96 More literally, "public opining."

They must appear thus, because they want to think, and because a contrary view and a confused one, probably indeed, disturbs their thinking with the trumpet blast of a sound mixed with the glory of war, but before all else, because they want to believe in that which is German and to recognize in this belief their strength [Kraft]. These believing ones are not to be blamed if they very much from the distance and from above look down on the land of their promises! They shy away from the experiences that the well-wishing foreigner exposes if he now lives among Germans and is compelled to wonder how little German life corresponds to those great individuals, works, and actions that he, in his well-wishing, had learned to honor as the authentically German. Whenever the German cannot elevate himself into the great he makes less than a mediocre impression. Even the famous German science, in which a number of the most useful domestic and familial virtues, loyalty, self-limitation, diligence, modesty, purity, appear raised up into freer air and at the same time transfigured, is still in no way the result of these virtues; considered up close [aus der Nähe betrachtet] the motive force [Motiv] driving toward unlimited knowledge looks in Germany like a lack, a defect, resembling much more a gap than a superfluity of strength [Kräften], almost like the result of a needy, formless, unlively life and even like a flight from moral smallness and wickedness, to which the German, without such diversions, is subjugated and which also, despite the science, indeed still quite often within the science, breaks forth. Upon the limitation, in living and in knowing, the Germans understand themselves as the true virtuosos of Philistinism; if one wants to carry them over themselves, into the sublime, thus they make themselves heavy like lead, and as such lead weights they hang on their truly great ones in order to draw these down out of the ether and to their needy neediness. Perhaps this Philistine-complacency may only be the degeneration of a true [ächten] German virtue – a heartfelt sinking into the singular, the small, the most near, and into the mysteries of the individual – but this moldy and degenerated virtue is now worse than the most obvious vice: especially since one has been blithely conscious even now of this quality of hearts, to the point of literary self-glorification. Now the *"cultured"* [Gebildeten] among the well-known so cultivated [kultivirten] Germans, and the *"Philistines,"* among the well-known so uncultivated Germans, publicly shake hands and strike an agreement with one another, how henceforth one must write, make poems, paint, make music, and even philosophize, indeed rule in order neither to stand too distant from the "culture" [Bildung] of the one nor tread too closely to the complacency of the other. This, one now calls "The German Culture [Kultur] of the Present Day"; whereby it would still only be to be asked by which marks is that "cultured man" [Gebildete] to be recognized, according to which we know that his milk-brother, the German Philistine, without bashfulness, at the same time according to lost innocence, gives himself now to all the world to be recognized as such.

The educated human being [Gebildete] is now before all else historically educated [gebildet]; through his historical consciousness he saves himself in the face of the sublime,[97] which the Philistine succeeds in doing through his "complacency." No more the enthusiasm which history excites – which Goethe may have supposed[98] – rather exactly the blunting [Abstumpfen] of all enthusiasm is now the goal of these admirers [Bewunderer] of the nil admirari,[99] when they seek to grasp [begreifen] everything historically. But one must call to them: "You are the fools of all centuries! History will only make confessions to you that are worthy of you! The world has been at all times full of trivialities and nothingnesses: your historical lusts [Gelüste] reveal themselves as just these and precisely only these. You can by the thousands pounce upon an epoch – you will hunger afterwards as before and you will be able to praise to yourself your kind of "health." Illam ipsam quam iactant sanitatem non firmitate sed jejunio consequuntur. dial. de orator.[100] Everything essential, history has also not wanted to say, rather mocking and invisible it stood next to you, pressing into the hand of this one a state action, to that one a period [Jahneszahl], to a third an etymology, to a fourth a pragmatic spider-web. Do you really believe history can be reckoned up together like an addition problem, and do you hold your common understanding as good enough for that? How must it annoy you to hear that others explain things, out of the

97 Or, "the elevated."
98 See footnote 5 of *Schopenhauer*.
99 See footnote 6 of *Schopenhauer*.
100 See footnote 7 of *Schopenhauer*.

most familiar times, that you will never and by no means grasp!"

If now to this self-naming historical culture devoid of enthusiasm [Begeisterung] and to a philistinism hostile to and full of venom toward everything great yet that third, brutal and excited cooperative [Genossenschaft] comes – those who run toward happiness – thus there will be in summa such a confused outcry and such a limb-contorting turmoil that the thinker will flee into the loneliest wilderness with stopped-up ears and bound eyes – therein he may see what those never will see, where he may hear what resounds to him out of all the depths of nature and down from the stars. Here he confers with the problems hovering near to him, whose voices ring out to be sure, just as much cheerless-fearful [ungemütlich-furchtbar] as unhistorical-eternal. The weak flee backwards before their cold breath, and the calculating run right through them without noticing them. But it comes out worst with them for the "cultured" [Gebildeten], who occasionally gives himself serious trouble: for him these ghosts [Gespenster] metamorphose into concept webs [Begriffsgespinnste] and hollow, sound images. Grasping after them, he fancies to have philosophy, in order to seek after them, he clambers around in the so-called history of philosophy – and if he finally has accumulated a whole cloudbank of such templates and abstractions, thus it may befall him that a true thinker blocks his way and – blows it away. Desperate inconvenience, to meddle with philosophy as a "cultured" man! From time to time indeed it appears to him as if the impossible combination that now boasts of itself as "Culture" [Kultur], has become possible; any hermaphroditic creature dances[101] and ogles around between both spheres and confounds the fantasy on this side and on that. But in the meantime the Germans are, if they do not want to let themselves be confounded, to be given one recommendation – they may all together ask what they now name "culture" [Bildung]: is this the hoped-for German culture [Kultur], so serious and creative, so redeeming for the German spirit, so purifying for German virtues, that their single philosopher in this century, Arthur Schopenhauer, should have to profess [bekennen] it? Here you have the philosopher – now seek the culture [Kultur] belonging to him! And if you are able to foresee what kind of culture [Kultur] that must be,

101 Or, "frisks."

which would correspond to such a philosopher, now thus you have, in this foreseeing, already, over all your culture [Bildung] and over you yourselves – passed judgment.

11. Compare paragraph 1. (*P I* 20, 133.)

Whoever now, as a well-meaning foreigner lives among the Germans will be struck with wonder [verwundert] how little German life corresponds to those great individuals & works that he, in his well-wishing, had learned to revere as the authentically German. Whenever the German cannot elevate himself into the great he makes more than a mediocre impression: he is then not brave, he is soft & not graceful, he thinks badly, he cannot stand, sit, & go. Whoever does not know him as the elevated,[102] that one knows him as the shabby. German science, as soon as one looks away from the few who advanced it in a struggle with their time, rests in its whole breadth upon these low qualities & gifts – you may point to any place elevated, thus is the elevated impossible under the ochlocracy[103] of the republic of scholars. The elevated wants namely to raise the Germans over themselves: whereas they make themselves as heavy as lead – they are "complacent."

12. Compare paragraph 2. (*P I* 20, 186.)

History will only make confessions to you that are *worthy* of you! The world has been at all times full of trivialities and nothingnesses: your historical beginnings reveal themselves as just these. You can by the thousands pounce upon an epoch and root it up with your common human understanding – everything essential, it has not wanted to say to you, rather mocking and invisible it stood next to you, pressing into the hand of one a period [Jahneszahl], to that one an etymology, to one, etc. You are the fools of all centuries. You want to make an addition problem out of history and believe that were precisely good enough. How must it annoy you to hear that others explain things, out of the most familiar times, that you will never and by no means be able to grasp.

102 Or, "the sublime."
103 Rule by the mob.

13. Compare paragraph 3. (*P I* 20, 117.)

One must be released from the cultural slime that now lies over all problems.

Here he confers with the great problems, whose voices ring out to be sure, just as much cheerless-fearful [ungemütlich-furchtbar] as unhistorical-eternal. The weak flee backwards before them, and the calculating run right through them without noticing them. But it comes out worst with them for the cultured [Gebildeten]: for him these ghosts [Gespenster] metamorphose into concept webs [Begriffsgespinnste] and hollow sounds, sound images. He fancies them, whereas he indeed only flirts, if he now with panting breast on abstractions he pushes forth before himself, seeking around after every conceptual temple in the so-called history of philosophy, upon such templates thus it may befall him that a true thinker comes into[104] his way & – blows it away.

14. Compare paragraphs 3 and 4. (*U I* 4, 114.)

Frequent experiences, of the kind described have really excited in Germany a feeling of a wicked kind of irritation against philosophy: whoever wants to get a hearing[105] as a philosopher will always do well.

From time to time indeed it appears, as if the impossible combination of that which now boasts of itself as "Culture" [Kultur] with philosophy has become possible – any hermaphroditic creature[106] between both spheres and confounds the fantasy on this side & on that. In the mean time the Germans are to be given one recommendation: they may all together ask what they now name: so serious and creative, that their single thinker in this century, Arthur Schopenhauer, should profess [bekennen] it? Here you have the philosopher – now seek the culture [Kultur] belonging to him! And if you are able to foresee what kind of culture [Kultur] that is, which would correspond to such a philosopher – now thus you have, in your consciousness, already passed judgment over it.

104 More literally, "comes against."
105 More literally, "come to a word."
106 A verb needs to be supplied here.

Homer's Contest

15. Compare the entire essay. (*Mp XII* 3, 2–13.)
What is humanity? There at bottom lies the idea that wants to be that which separates and distinguishes the human being from nature?

But the human being, in his highest forces [Kräften], is wholly nature and carries her uncanny double character in himself. His fearsome capacities are the fruitful soil out of which alone his noblest deeds and words grow, and those specifically designated as "human."

Thus the Greeks have in them a tigerish lust to annihilate and cruelty: strains which in the barbarically overgrown mirror image of the Hellenes, in Alexander, are very visible, but also in their whole history just as much so in their mythology, which puts into anxiety us who come up against it with the soft concept of modern humanity. When Alexander had the feet of the brave defender of Gaza, Batis, bored through, his body bound, living, to his chariot, in order to drag him around under the scorn of his soldiers,[107] thus is this the disgust-arousing caricature of Achilles, who mistreated the corpse of Hector nightly through a similar dragging around: but even this strain [Zug] has for us something offensive and horrible [Grausen] infused into it. We look here into the abyss of hatred. With the same feeling we stand, so to speak, also before the bloody and insatiable self-laceration of two Greek parties, e.g., in the Corcyrean revolution.[108] When the victor in a battle of cities, according to the *right* of war, executes the collected male citizenry and sells all the women and children into slavery, thus we see, in the sanction of a *right*, that the Greek thought [erachtet] of letting his hatred stream outward completely as a serious necessity: in such moments he alleviated in a fully pleasant way the feeling that had become compressed: the tiger hurried forth, a voluptuous cruelty looked out of his fearsome eye.

Why must the Greek sculptor stamp ever again war and battles in countless repetitions, stretched-out human bodies, whose sinews are swollen by hatred or by the wantonness[109] of victory, crooked wound-

107 See footnote 1 of *Homer*.
108 See footnote 2 of *Homer*.
109 Or "arrogance" or "high spirits."

ed, rattling out [their] dying? Why did the whole Greek world exult at
the images of battle of the *Iliad*? I fear that we do not understand this
"Greekly" enough, indeed that we would shudder if we should for once
understand it Greekly.

But what lies behind the Homeric world as the birth womb of
everything Hellenic? In *this* we will already have been lifted off and
away over the pure material melding by the extraordinarily artistic
determinateness, rest, and purity of the lines: its colors appear to us,
through an artistic deception, lighter, milder, warmer, its human
beings, in this colorful, warm lighting, better and more sympathetic –
but where do we look[110] when we, unled by the hand of Homer,
stride[111] backward? Only into night and horror [Grauen], into the product of a fancy accustomed to the horrible: which earthly existence do
these horrible Theogonistic myths [Sagen] mirror again: a life, over
which alone the children of the night, quarrel, lust, deception, old age,
and death rule. Let us think of the hard-to-breathe air of the Hesiodic
poem still condensed and darkened and without all the softening that
streamed over Hellas out from Delphi and out from numerous seats of
the gods: let us mix this thickened, Boeothian air with the dark volup-
tuousness of the Etruscan: then the reality would squeeze a mythic
world out of us in which Uranus, Kronos, and Zeus and the battles of
the Titans must be thought of as a relief [Erleichterung]: battle is, in
this brooding atmosphere, grace [Heil], salvation [Rettung]; the *cruelty* of victory is the peak of life's jubilation. And as in truth the concept
of Greek justice [Rechte] has developed itself out of murder, thus a
nobler culture takes its first victory laurel from the altar of atonement
for murder. Afterwards that bloody age cut a deep tidal furrow into
Hellenic history: the names of Orpheus,[112] of Musäus[113] betray the
results to which the uninterrupted spectacle [Anblick] of a world of
battle and cruelty pressed – to disgust in existence. But precisely this
result is not specifically Hellenic: in it Greece touches for once upon

110 The manuscript places a question mark after "look."
111 Nietzsche's manuscript here only has the first three letters of a word,
   "sch." He might also have intended "schauen," "look," backwards.
112 See footnote 4 of *Homer*.
113 See footnote 5 of *Homer*.

India. The Hellenic genius had ready still another answer to the question, "What wants a life of battle and victory?"

In order to understand it, we must set out from the fact that the Greek genius considered the at-one-time so fearsomely present drive as allowed and as entitled: the thought that a life with such a drive as its root would not be worth living was located during the Orphic turn. *Battle* and the *pleasure in victory* became recognized: and nothing so divides the Greek world from ours as the coloration, springing out from here, of individual ethical concepts, e.g., of Eris and of envy.

As the traveling Pausanias on his wanderings through Greece visited the Helicon, an original ancient exemplar of the first didactic poem of the Greeks, the *Works and Days* of Hesiod, was shown to him, inscribed upon lead plates and badly ravaged by time and weather.[114] Yet he recognized this much, that it – in opposition to the usual exemplars did *not* possess at its peak that little hymn to Zeus;[115] rather it began immediately with the declaration, "There are two goddesses Eris upon the earth."[116] This is one of the Hellenic thoughts most worthy of noting and is worthy to be impressed upon those coming in right at the entrance gate of Hellenic ethics. "If one has understanding, one wants to praise the one Eris just as much as to blame the other: for these two goddesses have a wholly separate kind of temperament [Gemüthsart]. For the one promotes the bad war and discord, the cruel one! No mortal loves her willingly; rather under the yoke of necessity they render honor to the heavy, burdensome Eris, according to the decree of the immortals. This one was born, as the older, to black night: but the other one Zeus, ruling on high, planted in the roots of the earth and among men as a much better thing. She drives even the unskilled [ungeschickten] man to work: and when one who lacks property looks upon another who is rich, thus he hurries to sow in a similar way and to plant and to appoint the house well: neighbor competes with neighbor, he strives toward prosperity: this Eris is good for mortals. The potter resents the potter and the carpenter the carpenter, the beggar envies the beggar and the singer the singer."[117]

114 See footnote 8 of *Homer*.
115 See footnote 9 of *Homer*.
116 See footnote 10 of *Homer*.
117 See footnote 11 of *Homer*.

The last two verses, which treat of odium figulinum,[118] appear to our scholars as inconceivable in this place [Stelle]: according to their judgment the predicates "resentment & envy" fit only to the essence of the bad Eris; the verses are to be designated as inauthentic and as winding up in this place [Ort] by accident. But for this they must have been inspired, unnoticed, by another ethic than the Hellenic: for Aristotle feels no offense in the relation of these verses to the good Eris.[119] And not Aristotle alone; rather the collected Greek antiquity thinks otherwise about resentment and envy than we do and judges like Hesiod, who at one time designates one Eris as evil, namely that one which leads human beings to hostile battles and wars against one another – and then again prizes another Eris as good, who as jealousy, resentment, envy entices human beings to action, but not to the action of a war of annihilation, rather to the action of the contest. The Greek is *envious* and feels this quality not as a blemish, rather as the effect of a *beneficent* divinity – what a cleft of ethical judgment between us and him! Because he is envious, he also feels with every excess of honor, riches, brilliance, and fortune [Glück], the envious eye of a god rests upon him and he fears this envy; in this case it warns him of the transitoriness of every human lot, he dreads[120] his fortune and offering the best therefrom he humbles himself before the divine envy. This idea [Vorstellung] does not, as it were, alienate him from his gods: their significance is therewith circumscribed in opposition, that with them the human being may *never* dare a conflict [Wettstreit], he whose soul blushes jealously against every other living being. In the battle of Thamyris with the Muses,[121] of Marsyas with Apollo,[122] in the touching fate of Niobe[123] appear the terrible opposition to one another of two powers that may never fight with one another, human being and god.

But the greater and more sublime[124] a Greek human being is, so much more naively does the ambitious flame break out from him, con-

---

118 See footnote 12 of *Homer*.
119 See footnote 13 of *Homer*.
120 Or "grants."
121 See footnote 15 of *Homer*.
122 See footnote 16 of *Homer*.
123 See footnote 17 of *Homer*.
124 Or "elevated."

suming each one who runs with him on the same course. Aristotle once made a list of hostile contests: among them the most conspicuous example is, that even one dead can still entice a living one to consuming jealousy:[125] thus namely A. designates the relationship of the Colophonian Xenophanes[126] to Homer and Hesiod. We do not understand in its depth his assault upon the national poet, if we do not think to ourselves, as later even with Plato, as the root of the assault the monstrous lust even to walk in the place of the overturned poet & to inherit his fame. Every great Hellene passes on the torch of the contest: in each great virtue a new greatness catches fire: if the young Themistocles, in thinking of the laurels of Miltiades could not sleep,[127] thus his early-awakened drive first unchained itself in the rivalry with Aristides[128] up to that singularly noteworthy, purely instinctive genius of his political action, as Thucydides describes it for us.[129] How characteristic the question and the answer is, if a great opponent of Pericles (Thuc.)[130] is asked whether he or Pericles is the best wrestler in the city, and he answers: "Even when I throw him down, he denies that he has fallen, he reaches his intention and persuades those who saw him fall."[131]

If one quite wants to see that feeling unveiled in its naïve expressions, the feeling of the necessity of the contest if the health of the state should endure, then one should think of the original sense of ostracism: as, e.g., the Ephesians expressed it with the exile of Hermador, "Among us no one should be the best: but if someone is it, then let him be elsewhere and with others."[132] For wherefore should no one be the best? Because thereby the contest is exhausted and the eternal basis of life of the Hellenic state would be endangered. Later ostracism received another position with respect to the contest, namely when the danger is manifest [offenkundig] that one of the great ones from

125 See footnote 19 of *Homer*.
126 See footnote 20 of *Homer*.
127 See footnote 23 of *Homer*.
128 See footnote 24 of *Homer*.
129 See footnote 26 of *Homer*.
130 This is Thucydides the general, opponent of Pericles, and leading member of the aristocratic faction in Athens, not the historian.
131 See footnote 27 of *Homer*.
132 See footnote 28 of *Homer*.

among the contesting politicians & party leaders feels enticed, in the heat of the battle, to harmful and destroying means and to dubious coups d'etats. The original sense, however, is not that of a vent; rather that of a means of stimulation: one removes the over-towering individual, thereby now again the contest [Wettspiel] of forces awakes: a sentiment that is hostile to the exclusivity of "genius" in the modern sense, but which assumes that, in a natural order of things, there are always *more* geniuses who reciprocally incite [each other] to deeds, as they also reciprocally hold [each other] within the borders of measure. That is the kernel of the Hellenic contest: it abhors and fears the dangers of solitary mastery, it requires, as a means of protection against the genius, a second genius.

Every gift must unfold itself in fighting: thus commands the Hellenic, popular pedagogy: whereas the newer educators have in the face of nothing so great a shyness as in the face of the unchaining of so-called ambition. Here they fear self-seeking as "evil in itself" – with the exception of the Jesuits, who are therein minded like the ancients and who appear to believe that self-seeking, i.e., the individual, is only the most effective agent, but its character as good and evil essentially [comes] from the goals after which it stretches out. But for the ancients the goal of the agonal education was the welfare of the whole, the state [staatlichen] society: every Athenian, e.g., should develop himself in the contest so far as to be of the highest usefulness to Athens and to bring the least harm. There was no ambition up into the unmeasured and the not-to-be-measured as with most of modern ambition: the youth thought of the well-being of his mother city when he, for the sake of the contest, ran or sang; he wanted to increase its fame in his own: he consecrated to his city's gods the garlands that the judges [Kampfrichter] reverently set upon his head. Every Greek felt from childhood on, in himself, the burning wish to be an instrument of the salvation of his city in the contest of the cities: therein was his self-seeking enflamed, therein was it reined in and closeted. Therefore the individuals in antiquity were freer, because their goals were closer and more graspable. The modern human being, on the contrary, is generally crossed by infinity like the swift-running Achilles in the parable of Zeno: infinity hems him in, he does not once catch up with the turtle.[133]

133 See footnote 30 of *Homer*.

But just as the youths to be educated would be educated with one another by battling, so again taught their educators in a battle among one another. Mistrustingly, jealously, the great musical masters, Pindar[134] and Simonides,[135] stride forth next to one another: in a contesting manner the sophist, the higher teacher of the Greeks, encountered other sophists: even the most general form of instruction, through the drama, was only conferred on the people under the form of a monstrous wrestling match of the great musical & dramatic artists. How wonderful! "Even the artist resents [grollt] the artist": and the modern human being fears nothing so much in an artist as the personal impulse to battle, whereas the Greek is only familiar with the artist in the personal battle! There where the modern human being smells the weakness of a work of art, the Hellene seeks the fount of its highest power [Kraft]! That, which, e.g., with Plato, is of special artistic significance in his dialogues, is mostly the result of a contest with the art of the rhetors, the sophists, and the artists of his time, invented for the purpose: "Look, I can do that also, what my great rivals can do; indeed, I can do it better than they: no Protagoras composed such beautiful myths as I, no dramatist such an animated and captivating [fesselndes] whole as the Symposium, no rhetor has authored such a speech as I put into the *Gorgias* – and now I reject that altogether & condemn all imitative art! Only the contest made me into a poet, into a sophist, into a rhetor!"

What a problem opens itself to us there, when we ask after the relation of the contest to the conception of the work of art! Let us take away, on the contrary, the contest form from Greek life, thus we see immediately in that pre-Homeric abyss a horrible wildness of hatred and lust to annihilate. This phenomenon shows itself unfortunately so frequently when a great personality was removed from a contest through a monstrously brilliant deed and was hors de concours[136] according to his own and to his fellow citizens' judgment. The effect is, almost without exception, an appalling [entsetzliche] one: and if one usually draws the conclusion from these effects that the Greek had

134 See footnote 31 of *Homer*.
135 See footnote 32 of *Homer*.
136 See footnote 35 of *Homer*.

been incapable of enduring [ertragen] fame & fortune [Glück]: thus one should speak more precisely that he was not able to endure [ertragen] fame without further contest, fortune at the conclusion of a contest. There is no clearer example than the final destiny of Miltiades. Through an incomparable result at Marathon [he was] placed upon a singular peak and raised far beyond. above every fellow struggler: he feels in himself a low, revenge-seeking lust awake toward a citizen of Para with whom he had an old enmity. In order to satisfy this lust he misuses his reputation, authority, the state's power, and civic honor, and dishonors himself. In a feeling of failure he comes upon honorless means of assistance. He enters into a secret union with the priestess of Demeter, Timo, and at night trespasses in the holy temple from which every man was excluded: as he has sprung over the wall and comes ever nearer to the holiness of the goddess, suddenly the fearsome horror of a panicky terror falls over him: almost collapsing and without reflection [Besinnung] he feels himself driven back and springing back over the wall he tumbles down lamed [gelähmt] & badly hurt [schwer verletzt]. The siege had to be lifted, the people's court awaited him, and a disgraceful death presses its seal upon a hero's career, in order to dishonor it for all posterity.[137] After the battle at Marathon the envy of the heavenly ones seized on him: and this divine envy catches fire when it sees a human being without any contenders, without opponents, upon a singular height of fame. Only the gods does he now have next to him – and therefore he has them against him. But these seduce him to an act of ὕβρις, and under it he collapses. Let us mark well that as Miltiades perished so perished the noblest Greek states as they, through service and fortune, had delivered themselves from the race course to victory, to the temple of Nike. Athens, which had annihilated the independence of its allies and punished with rigor the revolts of the downtrodden [Unterworfenen], Sparta, which after the battle of Aegospotamoi[138] made hold its superiority over Hellas in much harder and more cruel ways, have also, after the example of Miltiades, through acts of ὕβρις brought about their perishing,[139] as a proof there-

137 See footnote 36 of *Homer*.
138 See footnote 37 of *Homer*.
139 Or "decline."

by that without envy, jealousy, and contesting ambition the Hellenic state, like the Hellenic human being, degenerates. It becomes evil and cruel; it becomes revenge-seeking and godless – and then it merely requires a panicky terror in order to bring it to a fall and to smash it. Sparta and Athens surrender themselves to Persia, as Themistocles[140] and Alcibiades[141] had done: they betray the Hellenic after they had given up the noblest, Hellenic basic thought, the contest: and Alexander, that coarsened copy and abbreviation of Greek history, now invents the Persian Hellene, the Hellene of the whole world [Allerwelts-Hellene].

16. Compare paragraphs 5 and 6. (*U I* 5, 97.)

As the traveling Pausanias on his wanderings through Greece visited the Helicon, an original ancient exemplar of the first poem of the Greeks, the Works & Days of Hesiod, was shown to him, inscribed upon lead plates and badly ravaged by time & weather.[142] Yet he recognized this much, that it – in opposition to the usual exemplars, did *not* possess at its peak that little hymn to Zeus;[143] rather it began immediately with the declaration, "There are two goddesses Eris upon the earth."[144] This is one of the Hellenic thoughts most worthy of noting & is worthy right at the entrance gate of Hellenic ethics to be impressed upon those coming in. "If one has understanding, one wants to praise the one just as much as to blame the other: for these two goddesses have a wholly separate kind of temperament [Gemüthsart]. For the one promotes the bad war & feud, the cruel one! No mortal loves her willingly; rather under the yoke of necessity they render the heavy, burdensome Eris honor, according to the decree of the immortals. Now this one was born, as the older, to black night. But the other one Zeus, ruling on high, living in the ether, planted in the roots of the earth & among men as a much better thing. She drives even the unskilled [ungeschickten] man to work: & when one who lacks property looks

140 See footnote 39 of *Homer*.
141 See footnote 40 of *Homer*.
142 See footnote 8 of *Homer*.
143 See footnote 9 of *Homer*.
144 See footnote 10 of *Homer*.

upon another who is rich, thus he [hurries] to sow in a similar way & to plant & to appoint the house well: as neighbor he strives with neighbor toward prosperity. This Eris is good for mortals. Even the potter resents the potter & the carpenter the carpenter, the beggar the beggar & the singer the singer."[145]

The last two verses appear to our scholars as inconceivable in this place [Stelle]: according to their judgment "resentment & envy" fit only to the essence of the bad Eris: wherefore they make no bones [keinen Anstand nehmen] about designating the verses as inauthentic & as winding up in this place [Ort] by accident. But here, unnoticed, another ethic than the Hellenic has inspired: for Aristotle feels no offense in the relation of these verses to the good Eris.[146] And not Aristotle alone; rather the collected Greek antiquity feels & thinks otherwise about resentment & envy than we do & judges like Hesiod, who at one time names one Eris as evil, namely that one which leads human beings to hostile battles and wars against one another, & then again prizes another as good, who as jealousy, resentment, envy entices human beings to action, contests, not to war of annihilation. The Greek is envious & feels this quality not as a blemish, rather as the effect of a beneficent divinity – what a cleft of feeling between us & him!

145 See footnote 11 of *Homer*.
146 See footnote 13 of *Homer*.

Suggested Readings

On the Pathos of Truth

On Truth and Lying in an Extramoral Sense, Friedrich Nietzsche.

Friedrich Nietzsche on Rhetoric and Language, Sander L. Gilman, Carol Blair, and David J. Parent, editors. Oxford: Oxford University Press, 1989.

Philosophy and Truth, Daniel Breazeale, editor and translator. New Brunswick, N.J., Humanities Press, 1979.

Thoughts on the Future of Our Educational Institutions

On the Future of Our Educational Institutions, Michael W. Grenke, translator. South Bend, Ind.: St. Augustine's Press, 2004.

Nietzsche and the Philology of the Future, James I. Porter. Stanford: Stanford University Press, 2000.

The Greek State

Philosophie und Politik bei Nietzsche, Henning Ottmann. Berlin:Walter de Gruyter, 1987.

Nietzsche and the Politics of Aristocratic Radicalism, Bruce Detwiler. Chicago: The University of Chicago Press, 1990.

Nietzsche and the Philology of the Future, James I. Porter. Stanford: Stanford University Press, 2000.

Suggested Readings

The Relation of Schopenhauerian Philosophy to a German Culture

Schopenhauer as Educator, Friedrich Nietzsche.

Philosophie und Politik bei Nietzsche, Henning Ottmann. Berlin: Walter de Gruyter, 1987.

Willing and Nothingness: Schopenhauer as Nietzsche's Educator, Christopher Janaway, editor. Oxford: Clarendon Press, 1998.

Homer's Contest

Nietzsche, Politics and Modernity, David Owen. London: Sage Publications, 1995.

"Of Dangerous Games and Dastardly Deeds," Christa Davis Acampora, *International Studies in Philosophy*, 34, no. 3 (2002).

Philosophie und Politik bei Nietzsche, Henning Ottmann. Berlin: Walter de Gruyter, 1987.

Nietzsche on Tragedy, M. S. Silk and J. P. Stern. Cambridge: Cambridge University Press, 1981.

Nietzsche and the Philology of the Future, James I. Porter. Stanford: Stanford University Press, 2000.

Nietzsche and the Origin of Virtue, Lester H. Hunt. New York: Routledge, 1991.

"Nietzsche's Contest: Nietzsche and the Culture Wars," Alan D. Schrift, in *Why Nietzsche Still?*, Alan D. Schrift, editor. Berkeley: University of California Press, 2000.

INDEX

Achilles, 80f., 90, 90n, 126, 131
Aegospotomai, 92, 133
Alcibiades, 57n, 58n, 92, 134
Alexander the Great, 81, 92, 126, 134
Anacreon, 46n, 47, 47n, 106
Apollo, 55, 55n, 83n, 86, 86n, 98, 114, 129
Archilochus, 46n, 47, 47n, 106
Aristides, 88, 88n, 130
Aristotle, 35, 74, 85, 85n, 87n, 90n, 129f., 135
  Nicomachean Ethics, 35n, 85n
  Physics, 90n
  Rhetoric, 74f., 85n
art, 10, 12, 13n, 14, 14n, 19, 27, 36–42, 44f., 47f., 52, 55, 57, 59, 91, 94, 101–3, 105–7, 112, 114f., 132
atavism, 61f.
Athens, 89, 92, 92n, 130n, 131, 133f.

Batis, 81, 126
bellum omnium contra omnes, 52f., 52n, 112
Breazeale, Daniel, 18n

centaur, 42, 45, 105

Cercops, 87n
Cicero, 67n
  Definitions, 67n
Cleopatra, 49
communists, 48, 107
consciousness, 9f., 19, 27, 125
Corcyrean revolution, 82, 126
credo quia absurdum est, 65, 65n, 117f.
cruel, 34, 48, 50, 73, 84, 92, 107, 110, 128, 133
cruelty, 49, 71f., 76, 81–83, 108f., 126f.
culture, vii, 5–7, 12, 22, 28, 30, 32, 36f., 39–42, 44f., 48–50, 60–67, 69f., 78f., 94–96, 104f., 107f., 110, 117–25

Delphic oracle, 17f., 25, 25n
Demeter, 91, 133
Democritus, 67n
Demon, 18, 19, 26, 55, 114
Diogenes Laertes, 24n, 25n, 87n
dreams, 10, 18, 20, 26f., 45, 45n, 102f.

Egyptian, 108
Empedocles, 24, 97,99
envy, 9, 60f., 65, 72, 74–76, 83, 85f., 85n, 92, 127–29, 133f.

Ephesian Artemis, 24
Epicureans, 67n
Eris, 72–74, 83–86, 84n, 127f.,
  134f.
essence, 6, 9, 21, 23f., 42, 48f., 56,
  58, 63, 85, 95, 97, 99, 104,
  107–9, 114, 116f., 129, 135
Evangel of John, 48, 108

French Enlightenment, 54, 113
French Revolution, 54, 113

Gaza, 81, 126
Genesis, 77f.
genius, 5f., 10, 12, 40f., 56f., 59–64,
  80, 88f., 101–4, 111, 115f., 128,
  130
Goethe, 43, 67, 67n, 109n, 119, 122
  Aus Wilhelm Meister's
  Wanderjahren, 67n
  Faust, 43, 49n, 109n
  Maxims and Reflections, 67n

Hector, 81, 126
Hegesius of Magnesius, 81n
Helen, 52, 52n, 112
Hellenic woman, 117
Hera, 46, 46n
Heraclitus, 16–18, 17n, 24, 41, 88n,
  97–100
Herm, 57, 57n, 116
Hermador, 88, 88n, 130
Herodotus, 92n
Hesiod, 72–74, 79, 82 (Hesiodic),
  84, 85n, 87n, 128–30, 134f.
  Theogeny, 72f., 82
  (Theogonistic), 127
  Works and Days, 73, 84, 84n,
  85n, 128,134
Hobbes, Thomas, 52n, 53n
  De Cive, 53n

Philosophical Rudiments concern-
  ing Government and Society,
  53n
Leviathan, 53n
Homer, 52, 55n, 71f., 82, 87, 87n,
  111, 127, 130
  Iliad, 7, 52n, 55, 55n, 82, 86n,
  114, 126
Horace, 45, 45n, 67n, 105
  De arte Poetica, 45, 45n, 105
  Epistles, 67n

India, 76, 83

jealousy, 7, 52, 74–76, 80, 85n, 86,
  111, 129, 134
Jesuits, 89, 131

know yourself, 17f., 25, 98
Kronos, 72f., 75, 77, 83, 85n, 127

Lamiae, 109, 109n
Lycurgus, 56, 56n

Marathon, 91f., 133
Marsyas, 86, 86n, 129
Mephistopheles, 109, 109n
metaphor, 18f., 18n
Metis, 73f.
Miltiades, 87, 87n, 91f., 130, 133
Moses, 30n
Musäus, 83, 83n, 127
Muses, 83n, 84n, 86, 86n, 129

nature, 6f., 9f., 19, 23, 26f., 37–39,
  41–45, 47, 49–51, 53, 56, 68,
  70, 75, 80f., 99–107, 99n,
  109–11, 113, 120, 123, 126
Nietzsche, Friedrich, works
  The Anti-Christ, 62
  Beyond Good and Evil, 19n, 62

Nietzsche, Friedrich, *works* (cont'd)
  The Birth of Tragedy, 6, 93
  *David Strauss the Confessor and
    the Writer*, 65n, 67n, 68n
  The Gay Science, 62
  *On the Use and Disadvantage of
    History for Life*, 5n, 22n
  *On Truth and Lying in an Extra-
    Moral Sense*, 5n, 18n, 26n
  *Philosophy in the Tragic Age of
    the Greeks*, 5n, 9, 23n, 25n, 62
  Richard Wagner in Bayreuth, 67n
  Twilight of the Idols, 19n
  The Wanderer and His Shadow,
    82n, 84n
Nike, 92, 133
Niobe, 86, 86n, 129
nil admirari, 67, 67n, 119,122

ochlocracy, 124
odium figulinum, 85, 129
Oedipus, 42
Olympian laughing, 22, 96
Orient, the, 76, 83
Orpheus, 83, 83n, 127
ostracism, 79, 88, 130

Pater Seraphicus, 43
Pausanias, 84, 84n, 128, 134
Pericles, 88, 88n, 130, 130n
perpetual peace, 70, 76–78
Persia, 92, 134
Phidias, 37f., 46, 46n, 106
Philetas, 46n, 47, 47n, 106
Philistines, 60, 66f., 100, 119, 121f.
philistinism, 66, 68, 119–21, 123
philosophers, 12, 12n, 14n, 16–18,
    20f., 23, 24n, 27, 61, 63f., 67n,
    69, 87n, 96f., 99, 101, 123–25
philosophy, 6, 44, 54, 60, 64, 67,
    69, 104, 113, 122f., 125

*Philosophy and Truth: Selections
    from Nietzsche's Notebooks of
    the Early 1870's*, 18n
Pindar, 45n, 90, 90n
  Isthmian Odes, 90n, 132
  Pythian Odes, 45n
Plato, 12n, 13n, 16, 36, 57, 58n, 59,
    63f., 87, 90, 116f., 130, 132
  Gorgias, 91, 132
  Republic, 12n, 36, 57, 59n, 63,
    116f.
  Symposium, 58n, 91, 132
Platonic ideas, 13n, 20, 27, 117
Plato's perfect state, 57, 59, 116
Plutarch, 37, 46, 46n, 56n, 87n, 88n,
    106
Polyklet, 46, 46n, 106
Protagoras, 67n, 91, 91n, 132
pyramid, 50, 56, 102f., 110, 115

Rhode, Erwin, 4

Schopenhauer, Arthur, 13n, 60,
    62–64, 69, 123, 125
shame, 46–48, 65, 71,106f.
Sibyl, 25, 25n, 98, 100
Simonides, 90, 90n, 132
slave, 40, 44–46, 49f., 55, 104f.,
    108–10
slavery, 41, 48, 71, 82, 107, 109
slavish, 104, 115
socialists, 48, 107
Socrates, 58n
Socratic judgment, 59, 116
sophists, 90f., 91n, 132
Sparta, 56, 92, 92n, 115, 133, 134
Spinx, 41f., 47, 107
state, 29f., 34, 36, 40, 50–59, 61f.,
    64, 68, 79, 88f., 91f., 101,
    109–17, 122, 130f., 133f.
Strabo, 67n
  The Geography, 67n

strife, 71, 74, 78, 80, 83n
Sylvester's Night, 21

Tacitus, Cornelius, 68n
  Dialogue on Oratory, 68, 68n,
    122
temporality, 36, 39, 42
Tertullian, 65n
  De Carne Christi, 65n
Thamyris, 86, 86n, 129
Themistocles, 87, 87n, 88n, 92, 130,
    134
Thucydides (the general), 130, 130n
Thucydides (the historian), 57n, 71,
    82n, 88, 88n, 92n, 130
time, 6, 8–11, 22, 23, 28, 30, 33–35,
    45, 45n, 46, 48f., 53, 57, 60,
    63f., 68, 71, 73, 81, 84, 89, 91,
    95–97, 99, 102 105, 108, 112,
    122–24, 128, 134
Timo, 91, 133
Titans, 72, 75, 77, 83, 127
tragedy, 103
tree of knowledge, 7, 46, 105

tree of life, 7, 104
Trojan, 52, 52n, 111

Übermensch, 63
Uranus, 72f., 75, 77, 83, 127

vulture, 48, 107

Wagner, Cosima, 3f.
war, 52, 52n, 53n, 54–57, 66,
    71–74, 76f., 79, 82, 84, 86,
    111–15, 118, 121, 126, 128f.,
    134f.
work, 36–38, 41, 44–49, 56, 104–8,
    115

Xenophanes, 87, 87n, 130
Xenophon, 47n, 92n
  Oeconomicus, 47n
  Hellenika, 92n

Zeno, 80, 90, 90n, 131
Zeus, 25, 37f., 46, 46n, 72–75, 77,
    83f., 84n, 85n, 106, 127f., 134